# Skinks Liz

## Skinks and Blue Tongued Skinks care.

## Habitat, diet, health, common myths, diseases and where to buy skinks all included.

by

Elliott Lang

Published by IMB Publishing 2013

# Table of Contents

# Foreword

For people who are interested in pets that go a little bit beyond the norm, reptiles are a natural choice. Dogs and cats are wonderful pets, but they do not suit everyone, and that is where reptiles like skinks come into play. Skinks come in a wide variety of shapes and sizes, and there are many different species that might make the perfect choice for you.

Though skinks are not as social as cats, dogs or rabbits, it cannot be denied that these animals make fascinating pets. They are ideal for someone who is looking for an animal that does not require much care, a child who loves things that are out of the ordinary, or a classroom pet that can be admired by curious students.

Skinks are a perfect "gateway" reptile. For people who love reptiles but are not sure if they are suited to their care, a basic beginner's skink is a great choice to test the waters. Skinks on the whole require less setup and maintenance than larger lizards, and they are more responsive than many snakes.

Skinks are not for everyone, but they might be for you! Check out what goes into skink care and whether this pet is right for you.

# Chapter 1) General Information

## 1) What is a Skink?

A skink is a type of lizard that belongs to the family Scincidae and there are more than 1000 species of skinks that can be found throughout the world. Skinks are distinguished from true lizards like anoles and chameleons due to the fact that they have no distinct neck. Instead, their heads flow smoothly into their bodies. On the whole, their legs tend to be shorter, and some skink species lack legs at all, though due to physiology, they are still classified as lizards rather than as snakes.

Skinks are found in environments that range from tropical to arid, and their bodies are superbly adapted to their climates. The longer a skink's legs are and the sleeker its body, the more likely it is that the skink is an arboreal species, one that lives in the trees. The monkey-tailed skink is one example of an arboreal species that is commonly kept as a pet. On the other hand, skinks that have rather chubby bodies and short legs are typically ground foragers. The blue-tongued skink is one example of a ground-foraging skink that is common in the pet trade. As the most popular pet skink, the blue-tongued skink will receive a great deal of attention in this book.

Like all reptiles, skinks are cold-blooded, meaning that they need to bask in light on a regular basis in order to maintain their body temperature. All skinks will need some kind of heat and light source in their enclosure, though how much heat and light they need varies depending on the species.

These reptiles are an excellent choice when you are considering a pet that lives in a tank, but it is important to choose the right one. Some skinks are perfect for first time reptile keepers, even young ones, while some of the more obscure skinks require more time, care and attention to detail if they are to thrive.

## 2) Lifespan

In the wild, skinks live fairly short lives. Although they are predators, they are also prey for a wide variety of animals, including snakes, birds, larger lizards, dogs and cats. In captivity, however, where they receive adequate nutrition and protection from predators, they are typically much longer-lived.

The rule of thumb states that the larger a skink is, the longer it will live. For example, some people keep golden skinks, which are about eight inches long and only live to be between 8 and 10 years, while the larger blue-tongued skinks can live to be upwards of 20 years old with proper care and feeding.

Of course it is important to remember that all reptiles and amphibians live longer with good care. Like any other animal, skinks do occasionally sicken, and it is important for a skink's owner to take appropriate action. Skinks often do not show that they are ill until the condition is serious. Prompt attention, whether it is through a change in the skink's conditions or a trip to a knowledgeable veterinarian, is an important part of extending the skink's life.

## 3) In the Wild

With more than 1200 species to choose from, it can be difficult to get a clear image of what a standard skink's life and habits might be like. Many skinks are omnivorous, and there are a fairly large majority of skinks that are solely carnivorous. They are opportunistic feeders, and they are just as likely to eat live prey like snails, insects and small rodents, as they are to eat road kill and scraps from the meals of larger predators.

They are quite shy in the wild, and though most skinks can deliver a sharp nip when they are cornered, they generally prefer to run away. Smaller skinks in particular are very fast, and given their dull coloration, it is very easy for them to be overlooked by humans.

While skinks cannot cope with low temperatures, they can be

found in every temperature, arid or tropical climate. Some live in trees, some spend most of their time in or around water, and some can only live in dry deserts. Skinks that live on the ground are often burrowers, digging themselves small hollows to rest during the night. The blue-tongued skink, for example, burrows poorly, and thus often looks for the dens of other creatures when it is looking for shelter.

Skinks are mostly diurnal, meaning that they are most active during the day. During the day, they hunt, bask, and spend a great deal of their time hiding from predators. They can be found by turning over rocks or by simply looking for good basking spots on the rocks. If you encounter a skink in the wild, you should leave it alone.

# Chapter 2) Types of Skinks

## 1) Blue-Tongued Skink

If you are looking for a blue-tongued lizard, Australia has you covered. With their large size, docile temperament and easy care requirements, the blue-tongued skink is a popular choice for a pet.

These Australia reptiles grow to be between 14 and 18 inches long, and they have been kept as pets for more than 30 years. This means that for the most part, the skinks that you see at the reptile fairs and at the pet stores are bred in captivity and will thus be far easier to tame.

In the wild, they are known to be quite shy, and though their diet is easily limited in the captivity and they can eat things like mealworms, crickets and fruit, they are quite omnivorous as well. They have been known to eat roadkill, other lizards and even small birds and fish in the wild.

This Australia reptile is a classic choice due to its easy care and the fact that it is quite common. It is very easy to find blue-tongued skink breeders and blue-tongued lizards for sale in pet shops. This is an Australian skink, and it can become accustomed to a wide variety of climates and conditions.

When you are looking at this brownish, black blue-tongued lizard, look for healthy specimens from a breeder who takes good care of his or her animals.

It is definitely worth noting that when people are speaking about blue-tongued lizards, they are generally talking about the Northern blue-tongued skink, scientifically known as *T.scincoides intermedia* and the common blue-tongued skink. It is this species that is the most common in the pet trade, but it is worth noting that there are several other species that are marketed under this name.

For example, the Western blue-tongued skink is noted for its dramatic coloring. It is one of the most striking varieties that falls under this category, and its hide is a beautiful gold that is striped with black.

The blotched blue-tongued skink is an Australian skink that was once quite common in the pet trade. Over the past few years, however, they have fallen out of favor. It is quite a shame, as this specimen is known for its splotchy black and gold body and its rather adorable stubby tail.

Another notable blue-tongued species is the Pygmy blue-tongued skink, also known as the dwarf blue-tongued skink. This species is quite rare in the pet trade, and as a matter of fact, it was considered to be on the verge of extinction for quite some time. It only grows to be between 3 and 5 inches, and it is also known for its trait of living in abandoned spider burrows.

## 2) Blue-Tailed Skink

While the name is reminiscent of the blue-tongued skink, the blue-tailed skink is another animal entirely. These blue-tailed lizards originally come from the South Pacific, and unlike blue-tongued skinks, they seldom grow longer than five inches.

Blue-tailed lizards are known to be on the skittish side, and their small bodies are quite fragile, making them a poor choice for young children when it comes to pets.

The question of "are blue-tailed skinks poisonous?" is one that is troubling for some people, but the truth is that the results are inconclusive.

While this distinct white-striped black lizard with a blue tail does have the vivid coloration of many poisonous animals, and while a few cats and dogs have sickened after eating the shed and twitching tail, this is still not enough to say that the blue-tailed skink lizard is poisonous.

The skink's bite is absolutely not venomous at all. When you are curious about the blue-tailed skink, make sure that you have a few solid years of reptile tending experience to care for them adequately.

3) Fire Skink

The fire skink, also known as the African fire skink, is a lizard that ranges between 10 and 14 inches in length. This African lizard is native to Guinea, Angola and Uganda, and it is a common site at both pet stores and at reptile fairs. The most striking fact about this relatively calm lizard is its bright coloring.

The fire skink typically has red, black and white dapples on its sides, and its tail is black speckled with white. This is a large, relatively docile skink, and it spends long hours sitting contentedly in place.

4) Golden Skink

A golden skink grows to be between seven and nine inches long, and it can live for eight to ten years with the proper care. This is a naturally docile skink, and though it may be a little skittish when it is first brought home, you will find that dedicated and calm handling can turn it into a social pet.

They are natural burrowers, and they appreciate bedding that can be thrown around and used for digging. Golden skinks seem to do best on large gravel or recycled paper. They are quite hardy, and they can be an excellent choice when you are looking for a family reptile of some sort.

One of the biggest appeals of the golden skink is its bold, yellow coloring. Males tend to be bigger and more colorful than the females, but there are instances of big, colorful females and smaller, duller males. They are fast growers, and some breeders feed the very young golden skinks as much as twice a day to keep up with their growth.

5) Schneider's Skink

The Schneider's skink is also known as the Berber skink, and it originally comes from North Africa and some areas of the Middle East. With their sandy-colored, smooth bodies, they blend well into their native savanna environment, and their backs and sides are often speckled with gold or orange.

Depending on the sex and the conditions, healthy Schneider's skinks can grow to be 16 inches long, and they can live for up to 20 years in captivity, though life spans of 12 to 15 years are more common.

These skinks have grown in popularity in recent years, and that makes it easier to find specimens that were bred in captivity and handled from when they were very small. If at all possible, choose a captive-bred animal over one that was brought in from the wild. This ensures that the animal will be accustomed to people and disinclined to thrash or bite.

## 6) 5 Lined Skink

The 5 lined skink, also known as the 5 line skink, is native of the Eastern part of the United States. It only grows to be between 6 and 8 inches, and due to its small size, it can be quite skittish and shy. This skink has a pale body with darker stripes running along its back, and the juveniles have bright blue tails. Despite having a few superficial qualities in common with the blue-tailed skink, there is no relation.

They are known to be very active and very wriggly, and though their care requirements are relatively few, it is typically recommended that this skink is not kept by novice reptile keepers or handled by small children.

Seeing as the 5 lined skink is a native species in the United States, there may be some legal issues with keeping them. They are usually permitted in areas of the country where they are not native, and they are mostly legal through the parts of the country where they are. It is worth your time and your trouble to find out about the laws regarding these black and white lizards in your state.

## 7) Orange-Eyed Crocodile Skink

The orange-eyed crocodile skink may also be called the red-eyed crocodile skink or the alligator skink. This small skink only grows to be about eight inches long, and due to its nervous temperament, it is typically not recommended for new reptile keepers.

It favors a relatively humid environment, and though its long claws make it an excellent tree climber, it cannot climb glass surfaces. It does not accept handling easily, and most people who own them simply choose to observe them rather than play with them. It is relatively shy and apt to bite.

## 8) Bermuda Skink

Bermuda skinks, also known as Bermuda rock lizards, are among the most rare skinks in the world. They only grow to be 8 inches long with a rather slim body. This brown or black skink is endangered, and it is one of Bermuda's protected species. It is illegal to own one, and if someone is trying to sell you a Bermuda skink, they are either lying to you or engaged in something in which you want no part.

## 9) Pink-Tongued Skink

The pink-tongued skink is actually related to the common and highly docile blue-tongued skink, and for the most part, care requirements for this lizard are very similar.

These lizards are rather slim, and they spend some of their time hiding in trees and bushes as well as scuttling along on the ground. When they are fully-grown, the adults can be as long as 18 inches, with about half that length consisting of their slender tails.

They typically live for between 10 and 15 years if they are cared for correctly, with some especially hardy specimens living as long as 20 years, though that is more unusual.

The only really tricky part of keeping pink-tongued skinks is that their diet consists mainly of slugs and snails. Most people who choose to keep pink-tongued skinks end up breeding up a colony of giant African land snails to keep their skinks fed. If you are thinking about choosing to add this particular lizard to your collection, be aware that you will likely have to breed or order snails through the mail for more than a decade.

## 10) Sandfish Skink

The sandfish skink gets its name due to the fact that it burrows quickly through the soft sand, paddling through the debris like a fish cuts through water. This is one of the species that is frequently housed on sand.

This is a rather small lizard, topping out at 8 inches. It tends to live for 10 years, and though you should keep an eye on possible impaction if you house it on sand, it is generally a fairly hardy lizard.

It is quite attractive, with a yellow body and dark tan bands laid across its back, and its eyes and nostrils are on the small side, to keep sand out of them. Though they are increasingly popular at reptile shows and at pet shops, most specimens are still caught in the wild. This type of skink is difficult to breed in captivity, so do not expect to acquire a pair and to start breeding them.

## 11) Eastern Water Skink

When you are looking for a medium sized skink that tops out around 11 inches in length, you may appreciate the Eastern water skink. These handsome black and white lizards are very fast and very active.

Their bodies are black, and while their sides are speckled with white and their bellies are white, they have lovely greenish-gold spots on their back. They are very territorial lizards, and in many ways, they are somewhat delicate. They are great for an intermediate reptile keeper who is looking for something interesting.

## 12) Bobtail Skink

The bobtail skink is also occasionally known as the bobtail lizard, the boggi, the pine cone lizard and the shingleback skink, and it is an Australian skink that is native to very hot, dry environments.

Instead of having a long and graceful tail like other skinks, their tails are short and stubby. In many ways, it mimics their short, blunt heads in shape. Sometimes, predators will confuse which end of the skink is which, giving it more time to get away.

They are thought to mate for life, something that is on the rare side for reptiles, and this means that they can be kept in mated pairs. They can grow to be almost 18 inches long, but they must always be kept in very warm environments. Like other types of skinks, they have long bright blue tongues.

# Chapter 3) Common Myths

Skinks, like snakes and other lizards, are prey to many misconceptions. Some of these misconceptions are amusing, and some are quite harmful. Educate yourself on some of the common myths that are frequently told about these animals.

**MYTH: Blue-tailed lizards are poisonous.**

As a matter of fact, when you think of blue-tailed lizards- poisonous is the last thing that should cross your mind! When it comes to a blue-tailed lizard, poisonous attributes are not related to its bite.

Some dogs and cats have sickened when the try to eat these animals, but there is nothing poisonous at all about its teeth. Depending on the size of a given skink, its bite may be rather painful, but as long as you clean it carefully and thoroughly, it will be nothing more than a shallow cut.

**MYTH: Skinks are difficult to care for.**

While some skinks are very delicate and do need proper handling, most of the common skinks that you will find in the pet stores are perfectly easy to keep.

For example, when you are looking for a blue-tongued skink for sale, the blue-tongued skink breeders will be more than happy to tell you about how easy this lizard is to care for. The number of blue-tongued skinks for sale at reptile shows is always fairly high, and they are among the easiest skinks to care for.

**MYTH: Skink bites reopen on the anniversary of their occurrence.**

This myth is a complete fabrication. Skink bites can be painful, especially when you are dealing with a larger skink, but they heal just like any other minor injury. Most people do not even have any scars when the wound is completely healed.

**MYTH: Skinks can change color.**

Skinks are masters of disguise in that their coloration makes it easy for them to blend in with their environment. Chameleons are the lizards that are known to be able to shift their color.

**MYTH: I can leave a skink alone while I am on vacation.**

This is entirely wrong. Skinks need regular care. If you are going to be gone for an extended period of time, they need someone to come in every other day and to make sure that they have fresh food and water. Skinks cannot safely be left alone for more than a few days at a time.

If you are only leaving for two or three days, however, and you have automatic timers on your lights that are sent to turn on and off at 12 hour intervals, you can leave your skink for a short while. Feed your skink right before you leave, and then again when you return. Make sure that you do not leave your skink with water in the tank. If your skink defecates in the water and then drinks it, the infection that results from drinking stagnant, dirty water can sicken your pet significantly or even kill it.

**MYTH: There is no difference between skinks caught in the wild and skinks raised in captivity.**

It is true that skinks are not really domesticated. They have only been systemically and commonly kept as pets during the last fifty years or so, and that has not been enough time to give them the habit of being friendly with humans.

Even skinks raised in captivity retain all of the instincts of their wild cousins. However, it is important to remember that there are clear distinctions between a wild-caught specimen and one that was raised in captivity.

A wild-caught skink was captured in its native environment, whether that was the Australian desert or the forests of Asia, and shipped to the buyer, whether that was a reptile vendor or a breeder. They tend to be underweight, less healthy in general than captive-bred lizards, and in many cases, infested with parasites. A wild-caught skink also has no reason to be interested in humans.

On the other hand, a captive-bred skink has been handled since it was born. In the case of blue-tongued skinks, which are born and then removed from their mothers' cages very quickly, they typically get handled on the first day of their lives.

Captive-bred skinks are more accustomed to humans, and though they still have all of those wild instincts, they have never had a chance to use them in a life or death struggle for survival. They are accustomed to food coming from their owners, and they are usually much calmer in human company. On top of that, captive-bred skinks tend to be much healthier and less prone to be carrying disease or parasites.

When you are purchasing your lizard, make sure that you ask whether the specimens in question were bred or if they were caught from the wild and then shipped to your location.

# Chapter 4) Is a Skink Right For Me?

## 1) Why Own a Skink?

Skinks are excellent pets for the right people. People who own them generally feel that they are among the most calm and curious of the reptiles that are typically kept as pets, and after the initial outlay of cash for the skink's enclosure, regular costs are comparatively low. Depending on the species that you choose, they are simple to keep, simple to clean, and entertaining to watch.

## 2) Pros and Cons

There are several advantages to owning a skink. Firstly, these are friendly lizards, and though they can be a little snappish if they are scared, they are generally calm and placid pets. They are inexpensive to maintain, and compared to other reptiles, like snakes, they are friendly and exploratory. They are generally curious, and for someone who is looking for a pet lizard, there are several species that will serve as an excellent introduction to the world of reptile-keeping.

Some people love the reduced responsibility that is inherent with taking care of a skink. Though you need to feed a skink every day or every other day, you will quickly discover that it does not require the same care as a dog, a cat or even a gerbil or guinea pig.

Skinks are pets that are housed in enclosures, and they will not cause damage to your house and your property the way that a free roaming pet might. They remain where you put them, and you do not have to worry about them causing messes when you are not looking.

Skinks are also a good choice for people who have a bit of a collector mentality. Skinks are low maintenance, and though most of them cannot be kept in colonies, they will not feel neglected. As long as you are making sure that you can feed them, clean them and care for them, they do not need the same time that a mammalian pet does. Some people love having a few different species in their reptile collection.

However, it is important to understand what you are getting in to when you choose a skink as a pet. These animals can live up to 20 years old, and with that in mind, it is essential to look ahead and to figure out if you will be able to feed, house and care for an animal for that length of time.

Like all lizards, skinks can carry salmonella. Though this is easy enough to take care of by washing your hands thoroughly after handling the skink, it is worth keeping in mind for households that have small children or family members with compromised immune systems.

Finally, skinks are not mammals. This means that they do not exactly play with their owners, though some long-time skink owners believe that their pets do recognize them and respond to their voices. Skinks can deliver a sharp bite when they are aggravated, and they need regular handling if they are to stay calm and quiet in your hand. They cannot be conventionally trained.

Some skinks, particularly the smaller ones, are a little too nervous and delicate to handle on a regular basis. In this case, you may have a pet that you watch rather than hold or interact with.

This is something that is a little disappointing to some people, so make sure that you get species of skink that suit your requirements. As a rule of thumb, the larger the skink, the better a pet it makes. Larger skinks are known to be more docile and more prepared to interact with humans.

Sometimes it is difficult to find the right veterinarian for your skink. Skinks are still considered a bit of an exotic pet, and if you live in a rural area, it can be tough finding a veterinarian who has any experience with your animal at all.

While there are a number of ailments you can diagnose and treat yourself (See Disorders and Diseases), in many cases, you need a skilled medical professional. You may wish to scout out a good veterinarian before you purchase your skink.

When you are trying to decide whether a skink is right for you, there are a number of important facts that you need to take into consideration. Skinks can be rewarding pets, but as with any other animal, you must make sure that your household is both ready and willing to take on a skink's care requirements.

The United States has different licensing laws for animals that vary from state to state. If you are interested in getting a skink, make sure that you check the laws for your specific state. However, in general, the laws state that anyone may own up to four skinks without a license. If you end up owning more skinks of the same type or if you try to breed them, you are going to need to acquire an animal license of some sort, which typically comes with an annual fee.

All of the common pet varieties of skink are legal in the UK, though of course you should check your city ordinances to see if there are any exceptions. You may also consult with your local pet stores for local rulings.

## 3) Monthly Expenses

Though different skinks have different needs, it is possible to get a rough idea of how much it costs to keep a skink on a month-to-month basis. These expenses do not include the initial cost of acquiring the animal, its enclosure or the electricity to keep the skink's enclosure warm.

Your highest food costs are going to occur during the first six months, but even then they are not necessarily significant. During the first six months of their lives, juvenile skinks will eat every day or every other day, as they try to grow quickly and to put on as much mass as they can. Most people budget between 20 and 30 dollars or between 13 and 20 pounds for food that is fresh and nutritious.

Appropriate bedding can generally be figured at five dollars a month, and in general, when it is bought in bulk, it is even less expensive. Bulbs for heat lamps need to be replaced every few months when they burn out, and they are more expensive than standard light bulbs. Budget about 5 dollars or 3 or 4 pounds a month for a bulb, but remember that your bulb will not burn out every month.

These are the standard costs for maintaining a skink. It is also important to remember that your skink may need to go to the vet when illness strikes. It is generally a good idea to remember that the veterinarian may cost between 30 to 100 dollars or 20 and 65 pounds, depending on the visit, the veterinarian and the medicine or treatment that is required.

Though this might seem a little steep, remember that it is not nearly as pricey as a dog or cat might be!

## 4) Best Skinks to Keep as Pets

Skinks make great pets, but you need to consider which skink is going to be right for you. There is a full list of various types of skinks that are routinely referred to in the pet trade along with recommendations and warnings, but when you are looking for a quick guide, you will find that there are a few things to keep in mind.

When you are looking for an excellent basic pet skink, the blue-tongued skink is an excellent choice. The slow and placid blue-tongued skinks are excellent pets for a classroom, a child or a nervous first time reptile keeper. Do not confuse them with the blue-tailed skink, which is smaller and sleeker.

While the blue-tailed skink is also kept as a pet, it is a little more delicate than the blue-tongued skink. You will always be able to find a blue-tongued skink for sale. When you are searching out a blue-tailed skink pet, be sure to find a good breeder who will also tell you how to care for your animal.

Berber skinks, on the other hand, are less common than the blue-tongued lizards, but they are similarly easy to keep. They are a little hard to find, even at reptile stores, but as people start breeding captive specimens, they are becoming more accessible. Berber skink care is relatively straightforward, and the large Berber skink is an impressive addition to any collection.

The 5 lined skink, is a smaller specimen that is often seen at shows and at pet shops, but unless you are very patient, this skink makes a poor first lizard. It is very quick, fairly nervous, and it can be difficult to hold. Many people who keep these skinks simply leave them be.

# Chapter 5) Acquiring Your Skink

## 1) Where Should I Get My Skink?

Whether you are thinking about getting a blue-tonged skink or you are simply looking for 5 lined skink facts, the first thing for you to consider is where you can find the best skink for your household.

You can find skinks at the pet stores, but real reptile fans usually disdain the specimens that are sold at retail locations. In many cases, you can purchase your skink from the same breeders that supply the pet stores, and typically at a significantly lowered cost.

No matter where you get your skink from, always assess the conditions in which the vendors keep their animals. While reptiles do have a slightly dry, slightly musty odor, the area where the animals are kept should not reek.

The cages should be relatively clear of waste, and there should never be any rotting food in the bowls. Similarly, do not deal with an establishment that sees insects and parasites as a normal thing to have in the enclosures. All animals should have access to clear, clean water, with the possible exception being desert species, which may get their water through the food they eat.

One of the best places to get a skink is at a reptile show. Larger metropolitan areas have reptile shows on a regular basis, with some shows occurring every month. A reptile show brings together most, if not all of the breeders in a given area, and whether you are looking for a large reptile or a small one, you can find it there.

Be ready to face some serious crowds at reptile shows. They will be relatively busy and filled with vendors, breeders, people looking for new pets and people who are just stopping by to see the scenery. Do not purchase the first lizard that catches your eye. Walk around the exhibition hall and make sure that you see everyone that has a lizard of the species that interests you.

A good reptile show will let you know what is available in your area, and in addition to blue-tongued skinks, blue-tailed skinks and different types of Australian skinks, you can find rarer specimens as well. However, while reptile shows will give you variety, be ready to question the breeder closely on how they keep their animals, and be willing to be patient. These shows can be quite hectic and crowded, so be sure that you know what you want before you proceed.

You may also choose to purchase your reptile from an online vendor. While this can open up the selection of reptiles that are available to you, it is important to be wary when you purchase any animal sight unseen.

Make sure that you get a few photos of the specific skink that you are thinking of purchasing. It is not asking too much to ask for three or four pictures of the same animal in different lighting.

Unscrupulous breeders often take pictures of skinks in very strong lighting to give the animal a richer color than it actually possesses. If the online vendor is everything that they say they are, they will understand this concern, as this issue has become an epidemic in recent years.

Similarly, if you are willing to purchase a skink online, you should also be willing to pay the expedited shipping costs. The less time your new pet spends in transit, the more likely it is that your pet arrives safe and sound at your home.

Most reputable breeders also have a guarantee, especially if they are selling very young skinks or even older juveniles. At the end of the day, skinks are relatively primitive animals. Some young skinks will suddenly refuse to take food and starve, and some are prey to conditions that do not appear until they are a little older.

Look for a breeder or a vendor who has a guarantee. A 30-day guarantee that at least ensures you a replacement, if not your money back, if your new pet dies unexpectedly is an important indicator that you are dealing with the right skink breeder. Be aware that some skinks will simply refuse to eat or bear a genetic issue that ends up being fatal in very short order. Any reputable breeder will understand this.

In general, the thing to remember is that you should not feel pressured into buying a blue-tongued skink or any lizard at all. If someone with blue-tongued skinks for sale is trying to force you to buy a skink and you get a bad feeling, politely decline and walk away. There will always be other lizards, and it is not worth getting stuck with a sickly or even a dying animal.

## 2) Recognizing a Healthy Skink

When you are purchasing a skink from a reptile fair or a professional breeder, it is essential to make sure that you can recognize a healthy animal. Look for the signs of a healthy skink to ensure that you get a long-lived pet, and also check out the parents to make sure that the breeder is trustworthy.

Hold the young skink gently but firmly in your hands. If you have never held a skink before, ask the breeder to show you how. Generally, the technique used is to scoop the skink up from below, tipping it into your cupped hand. Most are fairly calm, but if you have one that is struggling, you can hold it in place by catching the neck gently between your index finger and the third finger of your hand, allowing its head to rest between them and its belly to lay across your palm and forearm.

A healthy skink moves quickly and gracefully, and its body should be supple and smooth. A mushy or lumpy body can be a sign of disease or malnutrition.

Lift the skink's tail to make sure that the anal vent is closed and clean. If there is any kind of mucus or discharge, choose another skink or another breeder. In general, though, one sick animal is enough to call the breeder's entire stock into question. Respiratory and gastrointestinal disorders are highly contagious, and at the first sign of illness, the affected animal should have been removed.

Similarly, check the mouth and nose for any redness, irritation or discharge, as these signs point to a respiratory infection. If you notice excessive drool, that is a sign that the animal might be sick, no matter what a breeder might tell you.

You also want to avoid purchasing a skink that is too skinny or too fat. A skink that is too skinny has skin that hangs loosely off of its body, and you can see its spine and ribs. A skink that is too fat looks slightly sausage-like, and its tail, head, feet and legs look too small for its trunk. While you want a good eater, you do not want a skink that is going to be slow and sluggish.

A healthy skink is one that has a rather sleek body, and when you gently squeeze its sides with your fingers, you will find it to be firm and muscular.

Your new skink should be healthy and lively when you purchase it. Do not trust a breeder who tries to sell you an animal that is lethargic or one that is obviously ill.

## 3) Getting My Skink Home

Many people have to drive a certain distance to get their skinks, and then they are faced with the dilemma of trying to get the skink home. Skinks are fairly hardy animals, but it is important to remember that they do have environmental needs that are present on any road trip.

As soon as you purchase a skink, go straight home. This holds especially true if you are on a long-distance trip, but it is still relevant if you are just a short distance away from home. The sooner you get your skink to your home and its new enclosure, the better!

Do not leave a skink in the car. Skinks are found all over the world, but that doesn't mean that each species can deal with any environment at all. Few skinks can deal with very low temperatures, for example, and the wide majority of pet skinks actually come from temperate zones, meaning that they cannot cope with the heat. Given the fact that temperatures in an enclosed car can mount to the hundreds on a sunny day, this could be very dangerous for a skink that cannot free itself.

Do not open the container that the breeder provided to you.

Depending on the skink species and depending on the breeder's preferences, your skink might be coming home with you in a cloth bag or in a small deli cup. You may think that the skink looks cramped, but the truth is that the small space will allow the skink to stay safer than it would be if it were in a large space where it could be thrown around.

Similarly, do not open the container to feed the skink or give it water when you go home. Skinks are not mammals, and they are fairly tough when it comes to going without food and water.

The key is to get your skink home as soon as you can while causing it the least amount of stress.

# Chapter 6) General Care

With so many pet skinks available on the market, it would be difficult, if not impossible, to create a care guide that was appropriate for all of them. The blue-tongued skink is one of the most popular out there, and in its general care requirements, you can see the shape that most skink care takes. If you are just starting out, a blue-tongued skink lizard is a great choice. They are docile, easily trained and large enough to be handled by children.

## 1) Basic Cage Requirements

The best time to set up a cage is before the lizard comes home. Too many people purchase a lizard and balk at realizing how much money is needed to give it a proper home. Though many of the items listed for a lizard's basic cage setup can be acquired used, it is not uncommon to spend between 100 and 200 dollars for your blue-tongued skink's basic set up. If you get your lizard's home set up before you bring it back, you will find that it is a lot less stressful for everyone.

When it comes to housing these lovely lizards, the thing to remember is that you can never have an enclosure that is too big. The black, blue-tongued skink is an animal that is used to having a lot of space in which to roam, and the more space the better.

The most standard setup for a skink is a glass tank. Though some sources suggest a fifty gallon tank for a blue-tongued skink, the volume of the tank is less important than the amount of ground that is available. Blue-tongued skinks are a terrestrial species. Unlike arboreal skinks that spend all of their time in the trees, blue-tongued skinks stay on the ground. Anything that is not at floor level in their cage is useless to them, and the more square footage that is available to them, the better.

One of the best setups for a blue-tongued lizard is to have a tank that is about a foot high, three feet deep and three feet across. This is the perfect size for a blue-tongued skink to grow into.

Though you can leave it on the floor, drafts can create a chill, so also look for a stand that will bring the tank up to waist-height or higher. You want to make sure that the tank is accessible for you so that cleaning and handling your pet is easy and straightforward.

You cannot leave the top of the skink's cage open. Even if the skink shows no desire to climb, an open lid can leave the skink vulnerable to other pets or to accidents. Use a screen mesh lid to ensure that your skink gets plenty of air while still being safely contained.

Remember that skinks in general, blue-tongued skinks in particular, are very curious and exploratory animals. Just because a skink cannot climb easily does not mean that it cannot rear up and nudge a loose lid open. The best tanks for lizards have a sliding lid or a locking lid of some kind. You can also choose to line the edge of the screen lid with specially designed lid clips, which latch the lid securely to the tank.

Take no chances, and make sure that each side of the lid has at least two clips. This may seem a little like overkill, but if a lizard can press its nose through a gap, it can often get enough leverage to push out the rest of the way as well.

The substrate is the bedding that you use to line the bottom of the tank. It gives your skink something to root around in, and it makes cleaning up after your animal a lot easier than simply scrubbing the tank out every time. There are a few different substrates that are fantastic to use, and a few others that should be avoided at all costs.

When you are looking for something simple and straightforward, you can bed your lizard down on several layers of paper towels. While this is certainly not harmful to the lizard, it leaves a little bit to be desired when it comes to visual appeal. Using paper towels as a substrate can be ideal if you are looking after a sick skink, when you want to check on its waste.

One of the most highly recommended substrates for reptile care in general is recycled wood pulp, which looks like shredded, fluffed gray newspaper. This product, marketed as Carefresh in many places, is very cheap and fairly healthy for your skink. The recycled pulp looks a little dull, but most skinks love to burrow in it.

However, if you are dealing with a dehydrated blue-tongued skink or any skink that needs a very humid environment, it is essential to note that as this material is essentially shredded and processed paper, it will remove a fair amount of humidity from the air through absorption. If you are dealing with a sick, dehydrated lizard, move to paper towels. Aspen is another great choice for reptile bedding, though you should be sure to get the large aspen shavings rather than the small ones. Smaller aspen shavings can be ingested by the reptiles, leading to issues with impaction. Aspen is a clean, dry bedding that is pale in color and quite attractive at the bottom of a reptile enclosure. Blue-tongued skinks love to burrow in it, and it is cheap and easy to acquire.

Do not use pine or cedar chips. There are oils in the wood that will affect your reptile's ability to breathe easily, and over time, bedding your skink on this type of substrate can lead to respiratory infections and skin irritation. If bedding has any kind of artificial or perfumed smell, it should be avoided.

Some people choose to bed their skinks in crushed shells or sand, but this is a poor idea as it leads to impaction. Impaction is a serious condition that occurs when lizards or snakes take a mouthful of sand with their meals. This grit gets stuck in their bodies, creating a hard mass in their abdomens, and it is something that can be fatal, especially when you are dealing with small skinks. Large gravel that is clean is typically a good choice, but it cannot be cleaned as easily as paper or aspen bedding, and it is very hard to disinfect. One exception to this rule might be the sandfish skink, as noted in the Types of Skinks.

Though recycled paper pulp is typically made from newspaper, the process has leached out the ink. Do not use newspaper as anything except a temporary bedding for a new pet, as the ink can affect the lizard's breathing and stain its feet.

While there is technically nothing wrong with using sphagnum moss as a substrate for your lizard, it is important to remember that one of the things that sphagnum moss is meant to do is to catch and hold water. This can improve the humidity of your tank to a certain degree, but too much water can make your tank too humid for your lizard's needs, and it can also start to rot if you do not keep an eye on it.

If you do end up using sphagnum moss in your skink's enclosure, be willing to check it on a nearly daily basis to ensure that you do not need to deal with mold or mildew.

Inside the tank, the lizard needs a large and shallow water dish. This dish should be dumped, wiped clean and filled with fresh water every single day. A shallow dish with a lot of surface area humidifies the enclosure, and it also gives your skink a place to splash and soak if it feels the need to do so.

Blue-tongued skinks are solitary creatures, and in the wild, they are often hunted by a wide variety of predators. As you might guess, this makes the skink more than a little shy. Too much time spent in the open where it can be easily seen is something that causes the skink quite a bit of stress, and this is where hides come in.

A hide is essentially an enclosed area where the skink can be alone.

Hides range from resin molded to look like rocks, to simple boxes with holes cut into them that allow the skink access to the interior. No matter what you choose to use for a hide, remember that there should always be at least two of them. One hide should be situated at the cool end of the tank while the other hide should be situated at the warm end of the tank (See Environmental Conditions). This allows the lizard to pick the spot that it likes best without needing to freeze or burn.

After you have created at least two hides in your enclosure, you are technically done, but you may find that you want to decorate your skink's habitat as well. There are many ways to do this, and you will discover that in many cases, going natural is the key. For example, take a look at the natural wood options at your local pet store.

Natural wood offers color to the enclosure's landscape, and you will also find that it gives your skink something rough that it can use to help remove the loose, dead skin when it is shedding. Similarly, you can look for large rocks in a wide variety of colors as well.

Avoid the temptation to bring rocks and branches in from the outdoors. In the first place, anything that you bring in from the outdoors can carry unwanted passengers like ticks or mites. You do not need to infect your skink with parasites on its first day. While there are some suggestions online that state that you can disinfect wood and rocks in your oven, this is something that you should actually avoid. If either the rock or the wood has air pockets inside it, heating it up can cause a serious explosion.

Though the chance of this occurring is fairly low, it is best to avoid it occurring at all. Rocks and wood that you pick up at the pet store have been heated slowly and in a controlled kiln, ensuring that it is safe to use and free of parasites. Another great way to get some color into your skink's home is to add some green artificial plants. While you could add suitable real plants, blue-tongued skinks are omnivorous, and they will eat them as fast as you can plant them.

If you are looking for places that have everything you need for keeping your skink, check http://www.kjreptilesupplies.co.uk/ and http://www.888pets.co.uk/ when you are looking in the UK. In the United States, check out http://lllreptile.com/ and https://www.reptmart.com/, which have both been in operation for quite some time.

Place your enclosure in a relatively quiet area of your home. Blue-tongued skinks are often as much the hunted as the hunter in the wild, and when your skink is getting used to a new environment, you will discover that it can be made shy and skittish by a lot of fast-moving shapes around the tank. Leave it in a bedroom or a study instead, and keep the room on the quiet side at least until the skink is more confident.

While some experienced reptile keepers do keep their blue-tongued skinks outside, this is something that should only be undertaken after years of reptile husbandry. Leaving your skink outside prevents you from being able to control their environment, and in a worst case scenario, can lead to your pet being eaten by a local predator.

## 2) Environmental Conditions

Blue-tongued skinks have a lot of leeway when it comes to their survivability in different temperatures, but you want to give them what they would be used to in the wild. This gives you the best results and the healthiest lizards. Essentially, your tank needs a cool spot and a warm spot, allowing the skink to bask as it pleases.

The cool spot in your skink's tank can range anywhere from the low 70's during the night and climb up to the low 80's in the day. Depending on where you live, it may be enough to simply keep this area of the tank at room temperature, though you should be careful about keeping the temperature of the house fairly regular in this case.

The hot spot in your tank is a little trickier, but once you get it set up, you will no longer need to think about it again. The hot spot needs to hover around 100 degrees Fahrenheit, and the way to get the temperature up to that heat is to use a heat lamp.

Heat lamps are available from home improvement stores and at pet shops, and the key is to choose the right lamp that will suit your animal. Use a 110 watt bulb and a 10 inch lamp to focus the heat in a tank that is 1 foot tall. A taller tank may require a 200 watt bulb to warm the area appropriately.

While undertank heaters and heat rocks are also used to warm up lizard tanks, you should avoid both of them. Undertank heaters are hard to install without smashing the cord between the edge of the tank and the floor, something that can lead to fires. Heat rocks put lizards in direct contact with their heat source, something that can easily lead to burns. A lamp that is set above the top of the screen is definitely the safest way to go about keeping your reptile warm and safe.

To make sure that your blue-tongued skink is getting enough heat in its tank, install a temperature gauge on the cool side of the tank and on the hot side of the tank as well. These gauges should be installed on the inside of the tank rather than the outside, as they will give you a more accurate reading if they are closer to what your lizard is actually experiencing.

There is a debate that goes back and forth on whether blue-tongued skinks need ultraviolet light. While it seems that they can survive without it, many breeders notice that their animals do better if they actually get at least a small amount on a regular basis. Take your lizard outside for a few minutes every temperate day to improve its digestion.

The other environmental condition that you need to keep in mind for the blue-tongued lizard's tank is the humidity, which is essentially the amount of water in the air. Blue-tailed lizards thrive in environments with between 30 and 50 percent humidity in the air. Typically, making sure that their large, shallow bowl of water is always filled with clean water is enough. Place a humidity gauge in the tank to check how high the humidity is. If conditions are on the dry side, consider gently misting the sides of the cage with water, though be aware that dampness in the cage can lead to mildew and bacterial issues.

### 3) Feeding

One of the first things that many reptile owners wonder is how often they need to feed their blue-tongued skinks. The answer is that it depends on how big the animal is. If you have a lizard that is less than a year old, feed it every day or every other day if it seems reluctant to eat. This is a vital period of growth in the lizard's life, and if you want to make sure that your lizard grows up to be sturdy and healthy, good nutrition at this early stage is essential. When you are dealing with an older animal, you should observe how often it seems to want to eat. In general, any blue-tongued skink that is more than a year old is going to need to be fed every other day, though some prefer to be fed less often.

Many experienced breeders do not feed their blue-tongued lizards in the same cage where they live. The issue is that when a lizard starts to associate opening the top of the cage with food, it will start to bite as soon as it hears the cage lid start to open. This in turn can make it a little difficult to reach your lizard when you just want to pet it or to clean the cage.

Instead of feeding your pet skink in its own cage, lift it up and bring it to a temporary cage. You will discover that in many cases, a large plastic tub with holes drilled into the lid will serve well enough. Drop your lizard into the feeding cage with its prey, and you can remove it later on after it is done.

The question of what blue-tongued lizards eat is a simple one; in many cases, it would be easier to talk about what they won't eat! The truth is that in the wild, blue-tongued skink eating habits are fairly indiscriminate. They eat whatever they can recognize as food, and that means that they are grazers, hunters and scavengers. These lizards are not known as fussy eaters, and that means that they are quite easy to take care of in terms of food. However, just because they will eat anything does not mean that they should be given whatever you have close to hand.

When you have a baby skink at home, give it a few days to grow accustomed to the world around it and then start offering it food. One of the great things about keeping a blue-tongued skink is that it is about as omnivorous as a human is, and it can eat many of the things that you find in your own kitchen.

Some people choose to feed their skinks food that is purchased in pellet form, but the truth is that far too few lizards will even recognize this as food! Head to the kitchen to figure out what kind of food your skink requires.

When you start prepping food for your skink, the secret is to remember that you should feed your skink about 60 percent fruit and vegetables and about 40 percent meat. Also keep in mind that there should be far more vegetables than fruit, as fruit contains a little more sugar than these lizards should have.

There are plenty of great vegetables out there for your skink. Remember that the more nutrients they can get from their vegetables, the better; this means that you should absolutely avoid feeding your skink things like iceberg lettuce, which many people refer to as crunchy water. Instead, choose leafy greens that are full of nutrients, like romaine lettuce, spinach and collard greens. If you have them available, your lizard will also enjoy things like kale and bok choy. These vegetables are fairly high in iron, something that your lizard does need. If you have issues remembering which vegetables are best, simply remember that the more colorful or dark the vegetable is, the more likely it is to be healthy for your skink. You'll also find that your skink adores squash of all kinds, whether you are looking at acorn squash, stringy spaghetti squash or butternut squash.

When it comes to fruit, there is a wide variety that your lizard will love. Basically, any fruit that you can pull out of the pile at the grocery store will work for you. If you want to keep things basic, remember to offer your lizard a few grapes with each meal, or diced bites of apple or chunks of melons. For something a little more exotic, look around for kiwi, papaya and mango. Juicy fruits will also help you keep your lizard hydrated.

When you go to feed your skink fruits and vegetables, you should cut them up into small pieces so that your skink can eat them and digest them more easily. Dice the vegetables and the fruits thoroughly, or use a food processor to roughly chop them into small and even pieces.

Finally, you need to make sure that your blue-tongued skink has enough protein. In nature, the skink will eat anything that it can get its jaws around and in some cases, they will try to bite off more than they can chew! When you want to feed your skink, you will discover that sticking with the lean meats are best. Chopped chicken breast is a good way to go, as is lean turkey and fish.

After your pet has its regular nutrition requirements taken care of, you can look at treats. Different skinks have different tastes, and while some go crazy for squash, others would love it if you fed them apples every single day. Most skinks, however, will love the chance to have more protein in their diet. When you want to give your skink a treat, you may wish to give them live or thawed pinkie mice or mealworms. While both of these foods function nicely as treats, they should generally not be a part of your blue-tongued skink's diet, as they are quite fatty.

Unlike snakes, who in some cases will refuse to take dead mice that have been frozen and then thawed out, most skinks have no such reservations. In the wild, they are frequently scavengers who will eat things that have been dead for some time. If you want to feed your snake young mice that have been frozen, you can thaw them easily. http://www.livefoods.co.uk in the UK is a good place to get mice, and http://www.rodentpro.com in the US is as well.

To thaw a single frozen mouse, fill a cup with hot, though not boiling water. Put the frozen mouse in a plastic bag, and then float the plastic bag in the hot water. This will thaw out the mouse in about thirty minutes. Touch the mouse gently when you think it is thawed. The mouse's flesh will be relatively pliant and yielding.

Never put a frozen mouse in a microwave. Due to the way the microwave heats water, it is possible that it will heat ice that may be inside a frozen mouse to the point where it can actually burn your snake. On top of that, you will also discover that mice warmed in a microwave can explode, causing an unpleasant mess.

Some people feed their blue-tongued lizards crickets, either as a protein or a snack. Remember that crickets on their own are not nutritious at all, and people who feed their beloved skinks live crickets right out of the mail order box are quickly going to be dealing with a malnourished lizard. In the United States, http://www.premiumcrickets.com/ is one place to get bulk crickets. In the UK, http://www.reptiles.swelluk.com/ is a good choice when you are looking for crickets and live food of any sort for your skink.

The truth of the matter is that crickets provide your lizard with very little beyond a bit of an entertaining hunt. If you want to make sure that the crickets that you give your blue-tongued lizard are nutritious, you will need to think about gut-loading the ones that you have.

Gut-loading essentially means that you make sure that the crickets contain nutrients before you feed them to your blue-tongued skink. Start by making sure that there is always some lettuce and a halved orange in the container with the crickets. This is a good way to make sure that your skink gets the nutrients that it requires.

If you are looking for an approach that is more measured, go to a pet store and purchase some supplements designed especially for this purpose. Any of the places previously listed for food and reptile supplies will carry reptile supplements, or check the Resources section for more information. These supplements are typically in liquid form, and they provide your crickets with all of the nutrients that they need in order to thrive. Simply apply the nutrients to the crickets in the manner recommended on the packaging, which might involve adding it to their water or their food. In some cases, where the supplement is in a powdered form, you can simply sprinkle it over your skink's crickets before throwing them into the feeding cage.

Your skink is an opportunistic feeder. It will eat what you offer it, and the best way for you to understand how much to give it is to watch it eat. A baby skink may only want a few tablespoons of food, while an adult may need about half a cup or more. Watch your skink while it eats, and when it is done, take the food away from it.

If you feed your skink in the cage it lives in, it is important not to let the food sit, or, in the case of live mice, roam. Crickets can be left in the cage, but for sanitation reasons, the rest of the food should be removed. As you get to know your animal, you will figure out how much it needs. Some blue-tongued skinks are very good feeders, while others tend to be more fussy.

When you want to save money on feeding your skink, one option is to raise your own crickets or your own mealworms. These creatures are quite easy to raise once you get everything set up, and you can get your starter animals from the pet store.

If you decide that you want to raise mealworms or crickets, you can make sure that they are well fed from the beginning, which will increase their nutritional value for your skink. Do keep in mind, however, that if you choose to keep crickets, you will at one point or another be forced to deal with rather loud escapees. Crickets are small and fast, and it can be hard to keep them all in their cage when you go to take a few out for your skink. On top of that, crickets are also quite noisy, and short of keeping them in another room, there is nothing you can do to silence them. Raising your own crickets is not strictly necessary, but if you think you want to collect or breed skinks, this is something that can keep your overhead much lower than it would be otherwise.

Once in a while, you will get a skink that is a little fussy about its food. It may eat some things and not others, or it may fixate on a certain type of food and refuse to eat anything else. If you are dealing with a picky eater, take the time to figure out what it likes best.

Some skinks go crazy for fruits and vegetables, and you have to find it a reasonable source or protein, while other skinks turn up their noses at anything but pinkie mice. Be patient, and simply offer your animal a wide variety of food. Some people deliberately offer their skinks food that varies on a regular basis when they are young so that they will grow up to be good eaters.

If you notice that your lizard is looking a little pudgy, it is time to put them on a bit of a diet. Keep the amount of food that they are eating the same, and instead make sure that you are only feeding the overweight adult every two or three days instead of every other day. Watch your lizard carefully for signs that it is getting pudgy. A healthy skink should be sleek and relatively narrow.

When you want to watch your blue-tongued skink eating, do not be alarmed if you notice that it does not eat right away. Some skinks need some time to get used to the idea of food, or even for their prey drive to be activated. If the skink noses the food and ignores it, give it an hour before you remove the food. It can take some skinks quite a while before they work themselves up to eating their meal.

Do not be alarmed if your blue-tongued lizard goes off of its feed. In the wild, these lizards are adapted to go for months without food if necessary. Check to make sure that the temperature and the humidity are what they should be, but other than that, simply be patient. On top of that, because these lizards go at least somewhat dormant in the winter, they will also cease to eat when the temperature drops. Missing a feeding or two here and there is nothing to worry about. Some skinks go several months without eating. Keep offering them food, and eventually, they will take you up on it.

## 4) Daily Care

When it comes to daily care for your skink, you will find that it is fairly minimal. However, though you have to do less for a skink than for a mammalian pet like a cat or a dog, the care that you do provide your skink is basic and essential. Do not get a skink unless you are willing to devote at least a small portion of every day to its care.

Start by emptying the skink's water, cleaning the bowl and refilling the water in the morning. Do not let water stand for more than 24 hours at the most.

Many skinks disdain water that has been left stagnant for too long, and on top of that, skinks will also urinate and defecate in their water, a sure recipe for illness and infection if the skink then turns around and drinks. Some people get around this by having a fountain in their lizard's cage, but it is not really hard to simply dump out the old water and fill it with fresh water every day.

Make sure that you replace your skink's water with water that has been rendered completely free of chlorine. Most home filtration systems take all of the chlorine out, but not all of them do, so be willing to check your filter's specifications. If your water filtration system does not remove all of the chlorine, look into dechlorination tablets that are available online or at any pet store.

Many reptile keepers simply dechlorinate several jugs of water a time and use those jugs for a few weeks. Do not offer your skink distilled water, as the lack of minerals in the water can lead to serious health problems.

Spot clean your skink's enclosure. Look for signs of defecation or urination and simply scoop up the waste and the substrate it is sitting on. A full tank cleaning, where everything is removed and disinfected, can be saved as a monthly chore, but a daily spot cleaning can go a long way towards keeping your skink's enclosure in good shape.

Handle your skink every day or every other day. The more you handle your skink, the more friendly it will become. If the skink is a family pet, make sure that it spends time with each family member. That way, everyone knows the proper way to pick up the skink, and they will not be worried about caring for it on their own should the need arise.

If you want to make sure that your skink remains healthy, it is often a good idea to make sure that you take your skink outside or at least to an area of the house where it can receive direct sunlight that is not filtered through a window.

Sunlight contains ultraviolet light, typically divided up into ultraviolet A and ultraviolet B, shortened to UVA and UVB. Both of these are thought to be necessary for proper bone development for lizards, and without them, metabolic bone disease can develop.

Depending on the day, your lizard will need to be fed. You can look at the Feeding section for more information on the topic, but it is worth mentioning a few feeding tips here. Some people do quite well when it comes to hand-feeding their blue-tongued skinks, but for the most part, it is not worth the risk.

People who do it successfully state that it strengthens the bond between themselves and their skink, but it can also cause your lizard to associate your hand with food. This in turn can leave you with a pet that is snappish even when it is not injured or angry, so leave the feeding and the treats in their proper place.

Check your lizard's cage conditions on a regular basis. Simply taking a quick glance at the temperature and humidity gauges in your lizard's enclosure can help you prevent things from going wrong. Prolonged issues with temperature and humidity can lead to serious problems for your lizard, but a little bit of vigilance can nip these issues in the bud.

## 5) Handling

While each individual animal is different, blue-tongued skinks are among the easiest to handle. When you look for a blue-tongued lizard for sale, one of the first things that a breeder or vendor will try to sell you on is that these lizards are great for kids. Compare this to the blue-tailed skink, which tends to be more skittish and more nervous. Some skinks are purchased specifically because of their ability to be handled, and when you are looking for a blue lizard or a blue skink, remember to think tongue over tail in terms of friendliness.

When you first bring your Australian blue-tongued lizard home, leave it alone for a few days. It is always best to have your enclosure set up completely before you bring your new pet home so that you can simply put it into the tank and leave it be for a while.

These black and blue lizards can get as stressed as any other reptile, and that means that they need a few days to adjust. Some people leave their skinks alone for upwards of a week, but in general, as soon as it has been exploring for a day, you can pick it up.

There are several things to keep in mind when you are looking to pick up this blue and black lizard, but across the board, the first thing you must always remember is that you want to keep it fully supported. That means that the lizard should have something underneath its front feet, its rear feet and the length of its body in between. If you leave the back legs unsupported, it will whirl its tail around looking for balance. While this is harmless enough in a baby skink, this is unpleasant and even painful if you are dealing with a lizard that is more than a foot long.

When you are scooping up these Australian garden lizards, consider the underarm cradle. Simply scoop the lizard out of its enclosure and deposit it quickly on your forearm. Your arm should be bent at a 90 degree angle and held close to your body with your forearm facing up. The skink's head can face your bicep or your fingers, and the length of your arm allows the reptile to feel supported. If you need to keep the skink still, you can lightly squeeze the head of a skink that is facing your fingers between your forefinger and your ring finger or between your thumb and your forefinger.

Do not be surprised if the skink urinates or defecates on you. This is just a standard risk of reptile keeping. The urine is odorless, and the excrement can be easily cleaned up with an antiseptic wipe. Blue-tailed skinks typically defecate or urinate when they start moving around, so be ready and seat the animal on a towel for a little while if you want to contain the mess. If you live in a temperate climate, you may let your lizard out to roam on the grass for a little while before you decide to hold it close.

The blue-tongued skink is known for being very laid back and sociable, but this means that it is sociable for a lizard. They will never interact with you the way that a dog or a cat will. However, some people do believe that their blue-tongued skink recognizes them and prefers them to others, and as your lizard gets used to you, it will definitely calm down.

While they are known to be among the most docile of the Australian lizard species, it is important to remember that blue-tongued lizards can defend themselves. The question of "is the blue-tongued lizard poisonous" is one that comes up frequently, and though the answer is a very firm "no," it can still deliver a nasty bite. If you take a look at the skink's mouth, you will see that it has no defined teeth, but it does have fairly powerful jaws. If you frighten it or aggravate it, you can receive a rather painful bite for your trouble.

You cannot train a lizard the way that you do a cat or a dog. Making a loud noise or punishing an animal this primitive does not work, and neither does rewarding it. Instead, simply stay calm and figure out why the bite happened. If you startled the animal, if you pinched it or caused it pain, that tells you about an undesirable stimulus that you need to prevent in the future.

On the other hand, if the blue-tongued lizard is simply unused to being handled, it simply needs to get used to you. If you are worried about bites, wear long-sleeved shirts or even a jacket, and cover your hands with tough leather gloves. Eventually, the blue-tongued skink will become accustomed to you, and you can dispose of the heavy coverings. Be aware that in the case of abused lizards or wild-caught lizards, this can take months.

To ensure that your skink remains friendly with people, handle it at least every few days. When you first get a skink, keep the interactions short. Your young lizard may only allow you to hold it for a few minutes before it starts to get nervous. Over the successive weeks, you can simply lengthen the amount of time that you hold your blue-tongued skink, getting it more used to you in general.

Remember that these Australia lizards, like all reptiles, carry salmonella on their bodies. Salmonella is a type of bacteria that can sicken healthy people and kill people with compromised immune systems, and it is especially hazardous to children and to those who are pregnant. Make sure that you wash your hands thoroughly after handling your skink. Use antibacterial soap and water, and make sure that you scrub under your nails. While this may sound very risky, the truth is that whether you are keeping a blue and black lizard, a golden lizard or a striped one, the risk can be easily contained. There are people who have kept reptiles for years who have never had a single problem.

Also keep in mind that while various members of the skink family can shed their tails to startle and distract predators, blue-tongued skinks cannot. Do not pull your lizard's tail or otherwise try to make it come off.

# Chapter 7) Miscellaneous Issues

## 1) Escapes

Escapes are just about every reptile keeper's worse nightmare, but even for diligent blue-tongued skink owners, they can occur. Simply forgetting to latch the cage as securely as you usually do can lead to an escape and some skinks make a break for it when they are in a less secure location while they are being fed or their proper enclosure is being cleaned. These blue-tongued lizards are quite talented when they do not want to be found, so your best bet is to start searching immediately.

First, make sure that you put other pets where they cannot harm the missing skink. Cats and dogs can seriously injure or kill even a fully-grown skink, so make sure that you put them outside or in a room that you have already searched.

Start by examining the room where the skink was last seen. If the escape was recent, the skink could not have gotten very far. While blue-tongued skinks are known to be quick when they need to be, they typically do not move very fast when they are out and about.

Check the corners of the room and the edges of the walls. Skinks like to stay close to cover when they are on the move. Check under your beds and under your bookshelves. Cave-like places are fairly attractive to them, especially when there is a lot of traffic.

These animals are not climbers, so you do not have to look on top of things, but be aware that sometimes, if the conditions are right, climbing is not necessary. Keep an eye on places where your skink might choose to hide, and be aware that if it is a relatively bold pet, it might simply saunter out when it is good and ready.

In your kitchen, be very thorough and look behind the stove and the refrigerator. These spaces tend to be rather warm, and skinks are automatically drawn to tight spaces. Move these large appliances very carefully, because if the skink is back there, you may crush it.

When you have started to run out of places to look, don't give up. If you have hardwood floors and no other pets, you may choose to sprinkle flour on the floor to see if you can pick up some tracks.

Another thing you can do is to crumple up some newspaper and leave it on the floor. The newspaper will rustle when the skink climbs over it.

One easy way to lure a skink back out into the open is to make sure that you put out some food a few days after it has escaped, and put that food in a place that you can easily see with a heat lamp focused on it. The heat lamp will warm the scent of the food and bring a hungry nearby skink out of hiding.

Even if it seems impossible for your skink to get into the basement, remember to search there as well. Basements oftentimes have insects, and as blue-tongued skinks are naturally omnivorous, they can hunt spiders, cockroaches and other insects for quite some time before they need more food.

You must also consider the possibility that the skink has gotten outside. Skinks can tolerate surprisingly low temperatures before they are harmed, but once they are outside, they are prey for a wide variety of animals.

If you have any pictures of your lizard, post wanted posters up in the neighborhood. Talk to the people that you meet to see if they have seen signs of a lizard in the area, and also ask for sightings of snakes, as many people do not look very closely. Give a call to animal control asking to be alerted if any lizards show up in the area.

Sometimes, skinks are at large for months before they are found again. While it is true that some escapes are never seen again, many others will show up again sooner or later.

## 2) Transportation

Given the fact that a skink can live for upwards of 20 years, you will find that it may be necessary to move the animal at least once, and perhaps even more than that. When it comes to blue-tongued skinks, you will discover that it is relatively easy to move them.

While these lizards can be shipped very carefully, you will find that it is far easier and far safer to simply move the skink with you when you are driving.

Do not place a skink in a pet compartment on a plane. It is far better to ship these animals, as the pet compartments on planes typically do not have the right kind of ventilation or temperature control that is required for the skinks' wellness.

Your skink's stomach should be empty when you are getting ready to move. Wait until it has defecated and then do not feed it more until the move is over. Ideally, the skink will have defecated no more than 24 to 48 hours before you are meant to leave.

When you want to move your skink, the first thing that you need to consider is a soft enclosure and a firm one. Start by placing your skink in a clean cloth bag. Tie the end of the bag in a knot or close it very tightly with string. In either case, you will find that your skink cannot escape.

Find a wooden crate and insulate the sides and the bottom with polystyrene foam. Glue a layer of polystyrene foam to the top as well to cap it off. Place your bagged skink into the crate, and secure the lid. Once you have done that, the skink is ready to be taken to its new home.

If you decide to transport the skink yourself, make sure that you keep it in the front of the vehicle with you. Do not put the box containing your pet into the trunk, as there is not enough ventilation there. Do not worry about water, because blue-tongued skinks are fairly hardy and can go quite some time without water, even if they would prefer otherwise.

If you decide to ship your skink, you can use the same boxing strategy. Look into the best local way to ship live animals. The United States Postal Service offer some limited services when it comes to shipping animals, but on the whole, it is far better to ship your reptiles through an insured carrier service or to simply find a way to deliver them yourself.

## 3) Finding a Great Veterinarian

Unfortunately, there are people in the world who do not believe that snakes and lizards deserve the same kind of veterinary care that a cat or a dog does. They consider reptiles to be disposable pets, but the truth is that if you bring an animal into your life, it is your responsibility to care for it to the best of your ability.

Though skinks and other reptiles are definitely growing in popularity, the fact remains that they are still considered exotics as far as pets are concerned.

Most veterinarians specialize in the disorders of dogs and cats, and after that, the animals most likely to be treated competently are rabbits and ferrets, though there are even problems there.

If you want to make sure that your skink gets the best veterinary care available when it is necessary, you are going to need to make a hunt for a great veterinarian. Start by talking to the breeder, especially if they are local to you. After that, start calling around.

The benefit of having a blue-tongued skink is that they are fairly common, and veterinarians who have experience with any reptiles at all will probably have worked with these lizards before. Things can get a little more difficult if you are having issues with a lizard that is on the rare side.

A quick phone interview may be all that you need to ascertain the veterinarian's experience. Call them up and ask them if they have worked with lizards before, and how much experience they have.

As with any health care professional, get a feel for them, and ask yourself how you will feel if you need to turn to them in case of an emergency. This is something that can influence your choice.

If you are having issues turning up a qualified veterinarian in your area, go online and ask around on the reptile forums. If you live in a medium-sized or large city, you will discover that people have all sorts of advice for you. Another avenue that you can use to conduct your research is the local veterinary medicine college or university in your area.

Paying for veterinary care is something that can be very

expensive, especially if it turns out that your skink needs surgery. For example, impaction, which is an issue that occurs when a skink has ingested sand and other debris and cannot pass it through its body, can require surgery.

Not everyone can immediately produce the money required to pay for the surgery, and it is important to have a plan before you find yourself in this instance.

Many veterinarians understand that accidents and illnesses happen and that not everyone is prepared for them. What this means is that things like payment plans are often available. Look around for a veterinarian who advertises payment plans in the case of large expenditures.

You might also be interested in pet insurance, but the thing to remember is that in many cases, pet insurance only covers cats and dogs. Look around for specialty pet insurance that is sure to cover your skink as well.

If there is any doubt at all, contact the insurance provider and make sure that your animal is specifically covered. If the worst does happen, the last thing that you want to find out is that you have been paying for useless insurance for years.

## 4) Solo or Group?

While some reptiles can be kept communally, it is generally recommended that skinks of any type are housed individually. Some species, like the broad head skink and the great plains skink, are known to be cannibals, and they will certainly try to kill and eat other members of their species. Most breeders only bring males and females together to mate, and then separate them again.

Some people have managed to house their skinks together, but no matter what precautions are taken, this is a risky endeavor. If you want to try, however, make sure that the skinks are of an equal size.

Even skinks that are not known for cannibalistic behavior will eat skinks that are significantly smaller than they are. If you happen to know the skinks' sex, avoid housing males together, as dominance displays and scuffles can quickly turn deadly. Two female skinks can sometimes live in harmony, as can a male and female skink.

If you are set on keeping skinks together, feed them in different enclosures. Ideally, you will remove one skink from the enclosure and place it in a designated feeding cage. Feed the skink there, and then, after replacing it in the main enclosure, repeat the process with the other skink. Skinks can be very competitive when it comes to their food, and scuffles can break out over food that is simply left in the tank.

If you want to try to house skinks together, remember that you should keep an eye on them. Even skinks that have lived together for years on end can suddenly attack one another.

If two skinks have a history of attacking each other, simply move to an individual cage setup. It is not worth the injuries or the death of a pet to consolidate their enclosures.

## 5) Bites

Even the most dedicated of lizard keepers will get bites from time to time. Most of the time, the bites are not serious and you can simply move on.

However, every now and then, a lizard will latch on to you, and when you manage to get it off, you will find that there is blood running. Wounds inflicted by lizards are fairly easy to care for, but if there is blood or sliced skin, it does require immediate attention.

First, do not worry because skinks are not venomous. Their bites carry no poison. However, it is worth noting that any skink that eats meat will carry a fair amount of bacteria in its mouth. This is something that can greatly increase your chances of infection if you do not take care of it right away.

Do not panic. Start by putting the skink back into its enclosure. It should go without saying, but do not try to punish your skink for its bad behavior. Skinks are not trainable, and the best that you can do is to simply make it comfortable enough that it does not feel the need to bite you in the future. Remember that it is difficult if not impossible to cause a skink discomfort without hurting it in some way. If a skink has bitten you, it is likely to be just as upset as you are, though it is not bleeding.

Remember to latch the lid when you replace the skink in the enclosure. Plenty of frustrated owners have just closed the lid in order to tend directly to their wounded hand or fingers, and when they have returned, they discovered that to further compound their issues, they now have a wounded skink on top of it all. Prevent an escape by carefully locking the lid.

Rinse the wound out with cold water. Cold water slows the flow of blood to the wound and causes the wound to stop bleeding more quickly.

Inspect the wound carefully. If you can see any white under the blood, that may be fat or bone. Most lizards cannot bite hard enough to do serious damage to a human, but sometimes, the reptile owner gets unlucky and the lizard just gets the most unlikely bite in. Remember that if you see fat or bone that you should take your wound to a doctor. An emergency room, a clinic or a doctor with an open office should be able to look after you. A wound of this sort may not close easily on its own, and it never hurts to be careful.

Get a piece of antiseptic gauze and press it to the wound. Hold the gauze in place firmly for about two minutes. If the blood has not at least slowed by then, the lizard may have nicked a blood vessel or worse. If the wound continues to bleed, got to a doctor's office.

Fortunately, most lizard bites are not so serious. After you have gotten the wound to stop bleeding, simply apply a good antibacterial ointment to speed healing, and then cover the wound with a bandage.

Every morning, remove the bandage, apply a fresh coating of antibacterial ointment to the wound and cover it up again. While some people believe that wounds need to breathe to heal, the truth is that the bandage prevents bacteria from getting into the wound and making it worse.

When you have an open cut on your hand, be extra careful to wash your hands after you have been handling your reptiles.

Some people get a little nervous around their lizards after they have been bitten for the first time. First, remember that bites happen all the time, and while they are painful, they are almost never dangerous. Second, remember that a skink that bites once is not necessarily a skink that will bite again.

If you are feeling nervous about handling your skink, wear leather gloves or canvas gardening gloves until you are feeling a little more confident.

## 6) Fostering

If you are thinking about bringing a lizard into your life, but you are still not certain that you are up to all of the responsibility, you may wish to consider fostering.

Fostering grants you the ability to house and care for a lizard without the challenge of being its permanent home. Reptile rescues are often short on both staff and space, and they will be more than happy to set you up with a skink that needs a temporary home.

If you decide to foster a lizard, you should not be asked to pay any of the expenses. Instead, you will simply be required to care for the lizard, to provide it with housing, to take it to veterinary visits as necessary, and to meet with prospective adopters.

This is a good way for you to see if having a reptile around on a long-term basis is right for you. Some people fall in love with the reptile that they are fostering, and they end up keeping it for the rest of its life. Other people realize that reptiles or even pets in general are not for them. Others decide that they like the variety of fostering, and continue on that way.

If you are thinking about fostering a skink, contact your local reptile rescue and give them your name and your intentions. In most cases, they will take down your information and set you up for an interview and a home visit.

The interview is designed to make sure that you know what is going on, what your responsibilities are and how to care for the animal that you are taking on. The home visit, which is typically very short and cursory, is simply intended to make sure that you have the right kind of space.

Fostering is an excellent way to make sure that a skink is right for you and your family without making a commitment that might last for decades.

## 7) Teaching Children to Handle Skinks

When the issue is handled correctly, children can gain a deep appreciation for all animals through their skink. However, it is important to remember that as with any pet, children need to understand what is and is not appropriate.

Remember that a child that is six or seven is likely to be too young to care for a skink appropriately. Even a child that is eight or nine should be watched carefully. For children around this age, a skink should be more a family pet than anything that they need to handle on their own. At around age ten or so, a responsible child can be expected to handle most of a skink's day to day care.

Make sure that your child understands that a skink is not a toy. It is an animal that can feel pain, and though blue-tongued skinks are relatively hardy, it is still quite easy for something as big as a human to hurt it. Impress upon your child that they have a responsibility not to harm animals that they are taking care of.

Another thing to keep in mind is that very young children have a tendency to stick their fingers in their mouths. This can be quite dangerous if you are dealing with a reptile of any sort due to the salmonella that they carry on their bodies. This is something that can put you off of owning a skink for a few years until your child no longer has this issue.

The best way to get a child accustomed to a skink is to pick up the skink yourself. Get it used to being held for a few moments. If it needs to defecate or urinate, allow it to do so.

Once the animal is calm, have your child sit cross-legged on the floor. If the animal squirms and your child loses their grasp on it, the skink will not fall too far.

Gently transfer the lizard over to your child, draping the length of its body over the child's forearm. Tell your child that they can touch the lizard gently, but remind them that most lizards do not care to be touched around the head. It is far easier and more soothing for a lizard to pet along its back. Some lizards can get twitchy if you pet them along their legs or too close to their bellies as well.

Make sure that your child is aware that getting bitten or scratched is a possibility, and be ready for that yourself. Blue-tongued skinks are known for their docility and their even temperaments, but they can be provoked into biting or flailing.

Inform your child that staying calm is essential when they are handling a lizard. Reptiles can feel when they are being held by someone tense, and this can make them more agitated as well.

Show your child how to wash their hands thoroughly after handling any kind of reptile, and let them know how important this is.

Make sure that a young child does not access the skink when you are not present. This can lead to the skink getting away, the cage getting broken and the child becoming injured, so be aware of the risks!

## 8) Training

The question of whether skinks can be trained is a complicated one. In general, the answer is "no." Skinks are not domesticated animals. They behave in captivity much the same way that they would in the wild, and they have never been bred for obedience the way that dogs and cats have been.

Smaller lizards are typically too nervous and skittish to train at all, but some people have had good luck with training larger lizards.

For example, some blue-tongued lizards can be housebroken. It involves keeping a close eye on the lizard and removing it to an acceptable spot, like the lawn or a certain delineated patch of its enclosure. Once it has defecated or urinated in that area, give it a treat. It will not understand praise.

Some people have managed to convince their blue-tongued skinks to walk on harnesses and leashes, but this takes time. Almost every leash set up that can securely confine a skink is too tight. It is preferable to simply put the reptile harness onto the skink and see if it will tolerate it. After that, you may be able to take your skink for very slow, very short walks.

# Chapter 8) Breeding

## 1) Sexing

Sexing skinks is very difficult. Unlike other animals, the males and females are not always clearly marked or colored. Instead, it is more common in the pet trade to simply guess at what sex a skink might be based on its size. Males are typically larger than females, but it is always worth recalling that there are both larger females and smaller males. In some species, the males are bolder, while the females are shier or more skittish, but there are definitely females that act more brashly and males that are more retiring.

One way to determine whether a skink is male or female is to look around the cage. If you see small white mucus packages left around the cage floor from time to time, you are probably looking at sperm plugs, which are only deposited by males. When it comes to blue-tongued skinks, you may notice that the female skink waves her tail from to side-to-side when she is in close proximity to the male. However, this is something that not all females do.

Even experienced breeders make their best guesses when it comes to sexing skinks, and if you are invested in baby skinks, you may simply need to house your skinks together and hope for the best. If you see one skink start to swell up with young, that skink is a female. For many species, that is the only way to tell the sexes apart!

There are scientific methods to sex skinks, but they are best left to veterinarians or someone who has many years of experience with reptiles. Probing occurs when a small metal pick is inserted into the skink's cloaca, an opening that is located close to the anal vent. An experienced person can determine the sex of a lizard by observing how far the pick travels into the body of the skink. Popping is a slang term for pressing lightly on the skink's body to invert the hemipenes, which are sex organs that are located inside the skink's body. Because skinks are fairly delicate in this area, it is very easy to hurt them when these maneuvers are attempted without careful guidance.

Unless you have a great deal of experience with reptiles, do not try to sex your lizard through popping or probing. Even the larger skinks can be very delicate, and at best, you can expect a sharp nip for panicking your pet.

## 2) Should I Breed My Skinks?

Some people would just love to have a baby skink or two, but the truth is that with successful breeding, you may get more than you bargained for! For example, with a blue-tongued skink, you may find that you are dealing with as many as 15 live offspring in a single clutch. Unless you can guarantee care for each lizard that is produced, you should not breed your lizards.

Similarly, you should not expect a great deal of cash out of breeding your skinks, particularly if they are of a relatively common species and coloration. Most breeders do it for the love of the hobby and their urge to share their favorite pets with the world. Skink breeding only begins to become even a little profitable when you start vending your specimens to pet stores and at reptile shows, and even then it is a fairly precarious business.

Finally, only breed your skinks if you have good stock to work with. Never breed animals that are frail or that regularly suffer from medical issues. To get good babies, you must always start with healthy adults in the prime of their lives. The older and more frail the parents, the more likely it is that the clutch will be significantly less healthy.

## 3) Breeding Rudiments

The ease with which skinks are successfully bred largely depends on the species. For example, the blue-tongued skink is relatively easy to breed. Not only does it make a great beginner pet, it also makes a great lesson for people who want to breed reptiles.

Compare that to red-eyed crocodile skinks, which take longer to come to maturity, and which are notoriously fussy when it comes to breeding.

Here you will find the basic instructions for breeding blue-tongued skinks. Not only is this blue-tongued lizard easy to find in stores, you will discover that their breeding setup is relatively straightforward. Make sure that you do not attempt to breed animals that are less than two years old. Females that are bred too young often have issues with their eggs, while small males that are bred to mature females often end up hurt in the rather violent mating.

The general overview for breeding blue-tongued skinks can be applied to many lizards, though there is a fair amount of variation regarding the specifics. The process starts with fasting, goes through a cooling stage, then a feeding/warming stage, and then a mating. The mating is repeated until the female is pregnant, a condition which is known as being gravid.

Two weeks before you start the cooling period, which is known as brumation, you need to stop feeding the lizards. Because skinks rely on heat to digest their food, a prolonged cooling period can lead to health issues in the skink due to the undigested food in its gut.

In nature, the brumation period involves a drop in the temperature, a decrease in light and a subsequent drop in the animals' metabolisms. While still keeping the skinks apart, slowly start dropping the temperatures in their enclosures until it is hovering around 50 degrees Fahrenheit. At the same, slowly reduce the amount of light that they receive in their tank to a period of about eight hours a day. This should take you about two to three months, though some breeders work faster.

After your breeding pair has been cold for a few months, start to gradually raise the temperature and the amount of light that they are receiving again. This simulates spring, the natural breeding season for this type of blue-tongued lizard. Start feeding the breeding pair small amounts of food, but do not be upset if they do not take it right away. Sometimes, they need the presence of live prey to trigger their appetite, so throw them some treats like live pinkie mice.

Clear all of the substrate out of the male's enclosure, or simply cover it with an old towel. During mating, the male's genitals, known as the hemipenes, are exposed, and the substrate can irritate them.

Place the female in the cage with the male. Do not place the male in the female's cage, as this can result in dominance battles. Even when dominance is not an issue, mating between blue-tailed skinks often looks alarming if you are not used to it. The male and female may roll over one another, there will be some scrabbling and some clawing. Watch carefully, and be ready to intervene if necessary. Eyes, feet and even tails can be ripped off during a mating, so step in if you see one animal get a hold of the other animal's body and refuse to let go.

In a successful breeding, the female shows her receptiveness by wagging her tail from side to side and allowing the male to mount her. The actual mating can take anywhere from a few seconds to a few minutes, and then animals will disengage on their own. There is no need to separate them; they will not get stuck.

If you have not observed a successful mating within 10 minutes, split the pair up and try again in a few days' time. The female may not have been ovulating, which means that she will not want to be mounted. Do not put the male back onto the substrate of his enclosure until you have seen his hemipenes pull back into his body. One common issue is that if the hemipenes take too long to draw back, they can get dragged over rough wood or substrate, injuring the delicate organs. At this point, the male's part is done. Male blue-tongued skinks have no part in raising their young, and they can even do them serious harm if they find them.

Observe the female over the next few months. Blue-tongued females may be pregnant anywhere from three months to a year, though a range somewhere in the middle is most common. The issue is that female blue-tongued skinks can hold sperm inside their bodies for quite some time. Until and unless they feel the conditions are right, they may not allow themselves to become pregnant. Instead, they will save the sperm until they feel that they are ready.

You can tell for sure that a female is pregnant when she starts to gain weight. During this period, feed the female every day or every other day. A formerly friendly female might also appear withdrawn or more aggressive when she is gravid. Try to minimize the stress in the female's life.

About a week before the birth, the female will stop eating and refuse even her favorite foods. She might also turn shy and reclusive, burrowing around in her substrate or spending a great deal of time in her hide.

Watch for heavy panting. When the babies are close to fully developed, they may push up on her lungs, causing her to be short of breath. Do not be surprised if you look away from the cage at night and suddenly see a baby skink in the tank in the morning. Some mothers even drop their babies over the course of a few days, so just because you see a few babies one day does not mean that she is done.

Do not be distressed to see a stillborn or some unfertilized embryonic sacs. This is a natural part of the blue-tongued skink's breeding strategy, where many young are produced under the assumption that several will not make it. The unfertilized egg sacs, known as ova, especially may be a little startling to you. They are often about the size of a large marble and bright orange in color. Allow the female to eat them if she wishes, as they are full of nutrients that were depleted when she gave birth.

One interesting thing to note about blue-tongued skinks in particular is that the females can carry unused sperm in their bodies for extended periods of time. This may result in a second clutch being born as much as a year after the last successful mating!

## 4) Caring for the Young

Blue-tongued skinks deliver live young, and once they are born, the mother does not care for them. As soon as you see the babies, it is a good idea to simply scoop them out of the mother's cage and deposit them in a twenty-gallon aquarium that is lined with paper towels or Astroturf. Do not put them on any type of substrate that has many small pieces.

For the first few months of their lives, baby blue-tongued skinks can be housed together. They are too young to be aggressive towards one another, and they are relatively social. If you want to keep them friendly for a little longer, handle them regularly. They should generally be removed to their own enclosures within two months of their first shed at the very latest. Some breeders find that keeping the babies slightly cramped helps them stay friendly. If they are kept in a cage that is too large, they may begin to mark out their own territories, something that in turn can lead to squabbles and even injury and death.

Newborn skinks are very independent, and they can be given the same food as the adults. For the first few weeks or so, simply feed them very soft cat food. After that point, you can start introducing them to the same food that you feed their parents. Feed them every day at first, as they are going to be growing very quickly. Provide water in the form of a very shallow dish. Just as for the adults, clean, clear water should be available at all times.

While they are still being kept communally, make sure that you do not feed them anything that is alive. Blue-tongued skinks have very sharp prey drives, and if it is triggered by a mouse or an insect, it may cause the siblings to begin attacking one another.

While blue-tongued skinks are not known for cannibalistic behavior the way that some other skinks are, it is important to remember that these are territorial animals and opportunistic feeders. They are used to roaming through the outdoors, and in the wild, two blue-tongued skinks who met and didn't mate would be apt to fight. In some cases, especially when there was a size discrepancy, the larger would eat the smaller. Do not risk realizing that there is one less skink in the cage than there should be.

5) Adopting Out Your Skinks

There is technically nothing wrong with adopting out the skinks around about the time of their first shed. While they can leave their mothers before this time, they are usually quite small and delicate. At this stage of life, some of them may still refuse food and end up starving to death, no matter how much you try to tempt them with food.

By the time of their first or second shed, baby blue-tongued skinks are eating much more reliably, and you can get an idea of their personalities. This is when most people start looking for homes for their skinks.

Do not think that you are going to make money from this endeavor. If you are breeding lizards on a small scale, you will never be able to charge enough to make back your costs or your time.

However, while keeping in mind the fact that you are not going to make your money back, it is generally a good idea to charge an adoption fee. An adoption fee is a small amount of money that is designed to make people think twice about whether they should really have a lizard. If the person balks at a 20 or 30 dollar adoption fee, you can generally tell that they are not in a great place and that they may not be the right people for your lizards.

Ask a few questions before you let someone walk off with a lizard that you have bred. Do they know what this skink eats, and do they know what temperatures to keep the tank at? If they are not sure of the answers, do not let them leave with a lizard until you have explained some of the care requirements to them. It is important for you to make sure that your lizards get into good homes if at all possible.

Similarly, do your best to make sure that your baby skinks are going straight to good homes. Ask the purchaser if they have a setup that is ready for the skink. Ideally, they should be able to deposit the skink into a ready enclosure as soon as they walk in the door. If they cannot do this, ask them to come back when they can. If they do not return at all, you can write them off as someone who was not going to take very good care of the skink in the first place!

You may also wish to see if any of the science classrooms in your town have the need for reptiles. Plenty of science teachers know enough about reptile keeping to be good owners, and you can be delighted that a lizard you bred is teaching young children about reptiles and how to treat them respectfully. If you have spent a fair amount of time raising your blue-tongued skinks, you can even offer to give a talk on these gentle reptiles.

When you want to adopt out your lizards, you probably should not bother going to a reptile show. Reptile vendors need to pay a certain amount of money for their tables, and unless you are a professional breeder, you are not likely to get your investment back or to adopt out every small skink you have. However, if you know someone who is a vendor and who is going to a show, ask them if you can throw some of your skinks in as well.

There are several reptile classified sites online that can help you find an owner for the animals that you want to adopt out. Kingsnake.com is one of the oldest and most stable reptile classified sites on the Internet, and you can find sellers and buyers from all over the world. It is customary to take on the cost of shipping. Faunaclassifieds.com is another site designed for reptile sale, and there is even a full section specifically designed for skinks.

When you want to sell your reptiles online, remember that you should always take good pictures. Even if you are selling four or five identical lizards, do not use the same pictures over and over again. Make sure that you have at least three picture of each lizard. Ideally, they will be taken in different light conditions so you can show people the true coloration on the animals that you are selling.

Be willing to answer questions regarding your lizards, and be wary of anyone who wants to bargain with you. If someone is trying to get out of paying you, be very wary of accepting their final offer. You do not have to sell your reptiles to anyone that you suspect will not take care of them! Selling your lizards can take some time. Be ready to care for your lizards until someone wants them. If you are interested in branching out into other types of reptiles, you might find people who are interested in swapping. Always make sure that you know what specific care is required before you go ahead and make that swap. As you can guess, caring for one lizard does not mean that you can care for them all.

## 6) Warning

Remember that breeding skinks in most states requires a license. Even if you intend to keep the baby skinks for yourself, you may still be fined if it is discovered that you have bred these animals without going through the proper channels.

# Chapter 9) Disorders and Illnesses

## 1) Burns

Burns typically occur when something has gone wrong with the heat source for a skink. It cannot be mentioned frequently enough that a skink should never have access to a bare bulb, and it should not have a heat rock inside its enclosure. Heat rocks particularly are responsible for many injured and dead animals, and they are not a safe choice for any reptile.

If your skink has come to be burned or blistered, you must first decide what kind of action needs to be taken. If the skin looks angry, is broken, or appears raw, that is a major burn and needs to be taken to an experienced veterinarian. The larger a burn is, the more significantly it can affect the animal's ability to live and breathe.

On the other hand, if the burn is relatively mild, you can attempt treatment on your own. Start by filling a plastic tub with between one and two inches of water, with the shallower depth for smaller skinks. Add povidone iodine, commonly sold under the brand name Betadine, to the water until it has a deep clear brown color. It should look a bit like strong tea. Let the skink sit in the water for about 20 minutes. If the skink defecates in the water, dump out the fouled water, disinfect the tub and replace it with fresh water and Betadine again. If a skink has a burn, it is of the utmost importance that the wound is kept clean.

After the soak, rinse the reptile with clear water and try to brush away any crusted blood or skin. Do not pull away anything that does not want to be removed. Be patient, and repeat this process once or twice a day for a week. If you do not see significant improvement in a week's time, it is important to take the skink to the veterinarian.

Take burns on skinks very, very seriously. Even a burn that looks small to you can take up a significant portion of a skink's surface area, and the larger a burn is, the more serious the condition.

2) Incomplete Sheds

Skinks, like all lizards, shed their skin as they grow. Younger skinks shed their skin every few months, while adults may only shed once or twice a year. A patchy shed is not a problem. Unlike snakes, which shed all in one piece, skinks shed their skin in small pieces. Depending on the size and the activity level of the skink, it can take the skink as long as three weeks to shed completely.

Incomplete sheds are sheds where large pieces of skin are still stuck to the skink's body, leaving it looking like it is peeling. Incomplete sheds can result in infections and irritation to the skink's skin, and if you notice that your lizard has been dealing with a shed for too long, it is time to look into what the issue might be. Sheds can hold infection next to the body, and if the skin won't shed around their feet, skinks can actually bite their own toes off. In some serious cases, skin that is not shed completely can constrict blood flow to the lizard's extremities, resulting in the loss of a toe or the tip of a tail.

First, do not peel the skin off yourself. The skin may be more firmly attached than you think, and pulling off what looks like loose skin can actually wound your pet. If the piece of skin will come off with a brush of your fingers, that is one thing, but if you have to tug at all, leave it alone.

Make sure that your pet has something rough in the tank to rub against. Skinks, like lizards, rub their bodies against rough things like stones or dry wood to peel their skin off. Make sure that there is something in your skink's tank that serves this purpose.

If your skink is having issues with shedding and there is something rough in the tank already, the issue typically has something to do with the humidity. The skin needs to be relatively moist in order to come off easily, and even if the humidity in the tank is ideal, your lizard may still need a little help. Mist the tank more regularly in order to ensure that the humidity is high, and consider adding a small amount of lightly dampened sphagnum moss into the tank to regulate the amount of water in the air. If that still doesn't help, there are things that you can do to help moisten the skin.

Start by simply placing a large container of water in the tank with the lizard to allow it to soak in its enclosure. Some skinks love water, and they will soon be splashing around.

Allow a larger skink to sit in a bathtub or sink that is filled with an inch or two of water for five to ten minutes. Pat the skink dry when it comes out. Do not leave a skink unattended when you place it in water with no way to get out. Skinks can drown in just a few minutes.

Soak a towel in lukewarm water and wring it out almost completely. Then wrap the towel around your skink's body and wrap a dry towel over the wet towel to keep the warmth and the moisture in. Hold the lizard in place for five minutes.

For smaller skinks that you cannot soak or wrap easily, consider purchasing a small resin hide and then placing a small amount of damp sphagnum moss inside. The moss holds moisture that is then trapped inside the hide, creating essentially a primitive warm sauna for your pet.

Be patient with your skink's shed. Humidity and friction are always the keys to fixing problem sheds.

### 3) Bitten-Off Toes and Cuts

If you house skinks together, they may be fine for years before violence erupts. Remember that unlike mammals, skinks do not recognize family ties or friendship. Even mated couples can and will attack one another. If your skink has been in a fight, it might result in toes that have been bitten off, scrapes and cuts. Though reptiles tend to heal quite quickly, you should take steps to help them out.

First, if you are keeping skinks together, separate them. While some people say that they have kept their blue-tongued lizards together for years, it is simply not worth the risk.

Fill a plastic tub with one to two inches of water, and add povidone iodine (Betadine) to the water until it has a pale brown color. Soak your lizard in this solution for between ten and twenty minutes. If the lizard defecates or urinates, however, throw the water out and start over again. Bathe the affected area gently, and if any scabs are ready to come off, lightly brush them until they do. If they are still fairly attached, however, leave them be.

After the soak, remove the skink and pat it dry with a clean towel. After that, apply a small amount of a triple antibiotic cream, like Neosporin, to the affected area.

Repeat the Betadine bath and the antiseptic cream application twice a day until you see that the wound has healed clean.

Every time you go to do the soak, check the condition of the wound. If it is running with pus, if it is red, or if it is swollen, this is a sign that infection has set in and that you should take your pet to a skilled veterinarian for stronger medication.

### 4) Mouth Rot

Mouth rot is a serious issue that affects many reptiles. Essentially, when the skink's mouth gets injured or inflamed, it can lead to a situation where the infection prevents the animal from eating or where it dies from infection. Mouth rot is a relatively common issue for skinks, and it is important for you to know how to recognize it and what to do if you see it.

The symptoms of mouth rot are subtle at first. The first thing that many people notice is that their pet is sitting with its mouth slightly open. Skinks that have this condition may have mouths that look moist or unhealthy, and as this condition goes on, their mouths and gums will start to become swollen inflamed. At the later stages of infection, the skink's gums and lips will start to bleed and show a marked red color.

As soon as you see any signs of mouth rot on your pet, it is important to start treatment. In the very early stages, you can often halt or even reverse the infection through changing the animal's conditions. Start by cleaning the cage very thoroughly and by laying down a new layer of substrate. Take care to replace the substrate and to clean the cage twice a week. This helps you prevent the virus or bacteria at fault from incubating in the skink's enclosure.

Make sure that you feed your skink foods that are more solid than watery. Juicy foods, particularly foods that are very high in acid, can harm your skink's mouth. Things like tomato juice and mangoes should be removed from your skink's diet and replaced with lettuce and berries. Cut these items down into very small shreds so that your skink can eat them in comfort.

Keep your skink's mouth clean by dabbing at it with a soft, dampened paper towel. Be aware that even the early stages of mouth rot can be painful for your pet. Hold it carefully and securely, but do not be surprised if it tries to nip you.

If you want to try treating your skink yourself, it is imperative that you avoid products that are too harsh. Some common antiseptic solutions like iodoform and hydrogen peroxide have been used in the past, but because they kill good bacteria as well as bad bacteria, they can slow healing and further weaken the skink. If your skink needs its mouth cleaned, start by significantly diluting povidone iodine, commonly sold as Betadine. When it is the color of a fairly weak tea, dunk a Q-tip into the solution and gently pat it onto the affected areas. Do this twice a day until the condition starts to clear up.

When you start to see blood or when your efforts are not resolving in improvement, it is time to take your animal to the veterinarian. Make sure that you tell your veterinarian about what your skink was eating and any changes that might have occurred. The more information the veterinarian has, the more likely it is that he or she will be able to help you.

## 5) Respiratory Infections

Respiratory infections are fairly common among skinks of all sorts, and even the most fastidious reptile keepers can find their charges affected. When you are concerned that your skink might be struggling with a respiratory infection, it is important for you to learn the causes, the symptoms and the treatment for this issue.

At the most basic level, a respiratory infection is a bacterial, viral or fungal attack on the animal's lungs. It can strike out of the blue, but in many cases, it is caused by issues in the skink's living conditions. For example, an enclosure that is too high in humidity can cause a respiratory infection, as can conditions that are too cool for the lizard in question.

If you have recently moved your skink to a new enclosure or simply moved house yourself, the stress that goes with it can weaken your skink's immune system until it sickens. Skinks kept in dirty enclosures are also at risk, as dust from their droppings can cycle through the air and end up in their lungs.

There are certain symptoms that always go with respiratory infections. It is generally recommended that you give your skink a little bit of attention every day so that you can note such changes when they start, rather than having a bad condition continue until it is dangerous. Watch for a drop in appetite and weight loss, especially if it is correlated with bloating along the skink's body. Similarly, the skink might be very fatigued, causing it to stop moving as actively or as quickly as it can.

One sure sign of a respiratory infection is labored breathing. You may notice that the skink breathes hard with its mouth open, or you may find that there is mucus coming from the mouth and even the nose. You may hear a clicking sound when you hold the lizard up to your ear, which is the lungs trying to work when there is mucus in them. The reptile might also sit with its head elevated to make breathing easier.

If you are housing your blue-tongued skink with other skinks, you need to immediately isolate the affected animal. Even two ill animals should not be housed together, as this can result in the infection being passed back and forth between animals that are struggling to improve. Some skink keepers do not even keep ill skinks in the same room as healthy ones. You should always clean your hands very well with soap and water when handling any kind of reptile, but be especially careful when you are dealing with ill skinks.

If you suspect that your skink is having a respiratory infection, make an immediate evaluation of the skink's conditions. Check the humidity, check the cleanliness of the cage and check the temperature.

Place the skink in a clean temporary cage and throw away all of the bed. Sterilize the enclosure and everything in it before you return the skink to its cage. You may also check to see if there is a draft coming in. If you placed the enclosure somewhere during the summer months, and now you are dealing with winter temperatures and winds, a draft might have appeared where before there was none. In some cases, this is all it takes to take care of a skink with a mild respiratory illness.

If your skink does not show immediate signs of improvement, it is time to go to a veterinarian. Only a veterinarian is capable of determining what type of systemic antibiotics your lizard might need, and they can also help you get more liquid into the animal as many cases of respiratory infection also involve dehydration. In some cases, a swab test will be taken to determine the exact culprit so that treatment can be more directed. Depending on your veterinarian, the medication prescribed may be injected, consumed orally or even inhaled.

A great deal of mucus dripping from the mouth is typically a later sign of respiratory infection. If you notice this sign before you see any others, take your skink to the veterinarian right away, because this may be a sign that your skink has ingested something that is poisonous.

### 6) Refusal of Food

Young skinks eat every day or so, while skinks that are fully grown adults may only eat two or three times a week. Skinks can go a very long time without food, and eventually, they will start again when they feel like it. If your skink has missed a few feedings, there is nothing to be alarmed about. For example, in the case of the blue-tongued skink, it is normal for them to go off their food for three to four months at a stretch. In the wild, this is quite normal for them, as the cold weather slows their digestion. Many skinks also start to refuse food when they get closer to breeding.

A few skipped meals is nothing to worry about when it comes to your skink, but if it goes on too long, anorexia can actually lead to a skink starving to death. If you have noticed that your skink is not eating, there are a few things that you can do about it.

First, make sure that the environment is where it needs to be. Skinks are cold-blooded, and that means that their environment needs to be a certain temperature with regards to their digestion. If the heat lamp has been flickering or if the enclosure is drier than it should be, this can put your skink off its food.

Try to tempt your skink into eating by offering it its favorite foods. If that doesn't work, look for some low-fat sugar-free baby food and smear just a dab on the skink's nose. Your skink may lick the offending substance off of its face and be reminded that it likes to eat.

Check the skink's mouth. Mouth rot may be present, and if it is painful to eat, the skink might stop entirely. Look for any evidence of parasites, like red or raw skin, or mites crawling in the bedding. These issues have their own treatment.

If conditions are good but your skink still refuses to eat, you can try giving your skink a bath to help it absorb vitamins and to hopefully encourage it to release waste. Start by filling a container that is large enough to fit your skink with a solution that is half water and half Pedialyte. Pedialyte is full of vitamins that can be soaked into your skink's skin, and the water can help your skink stay hydrated if it is not eating its regular diet of vegetables. Let your skink sit in the tub for about half an hour, and as it does so, spend about 10 minutes stroking your fingers along your skink's belly, moving from its throat to its anal vent. This is a good way to encourage your skink's digestive system to kick into gear. Do not be surprised if your skink defecates into the water. If this happens, wait a day and try to feed your skink again. If you do not see any immediate results, simply repeat this process twice a day.

Do not try force feeding your skink. Force feeding is a very stressful experience for the animal, and the stress that it causes is out of proportion to even the effects of anorexia. Force feeding any reptile can result in food going into the animal's lungs, which in turn can result in a fatal infection. A veterinarian should be the person making the decision on whether force feeding is necessary. Similarly, if impaction is an issue, adding more matter to the skink's stomach that it cannot expel is only going to make the situation worse.

### 7) Dehydration

Dehydration is typically a symptom rather than an actual issue in and of itself. Dehydration can result from poor conditions, parasites or stress, but no matter what the cause, the dehydration needs to be fixed. Some of the common signs of dehydration in skinks include; skin that feels slightly papery to the touch, eyes that are sunken into the skink's head, and a lower amount of activity than normal. One easy test that you can try on skinks in general to find out if they are dehydrated involves pinching a small fold of the skink's skin between your thumb and forefinger. If the skin remains where your fingers pulled it, there is a good chance that the animal is dehydrated. On the other hand, if the lizard's skin snaps back to where it was, this is a good sign that the lizard has enough water in its system.

If the lizard has simply been in a situation without access to water, rehydrating the animal is frequently as easy as offering it fresh clean water in a comfortable environment. However, if the lizard has an oral issue that is making lapping water difficult or if it is simply too weak, you can get the water into the animal through a syringe. Choose a syringe with no needle and use it to drip a few drops of water on the animal's snout. A half water, half Pedialyte solution can be used the same way.

In cases where every little bit of water helps, make sure that you give the skink a Pedialyte bath, as described in the section, Refusal of Food. You can also mist down the walls of the skink's enclosure with water, improving the humidity in the tank and creating a situation where the skink respires more easily. If the skink eats fruit and vegetables, you can offer them fairly juicy bite-size portions to help them rehydrate.

If the skink looks like it is having trouble breathing, if its eyes are dull or if its activity level has cut down significantly, it is time to take it to the veterinarian. Depending on the animal's condition, the veterinarian may have to use injections to get water into the skink's body or in the worst case scenario, the animal might have to be euthanized.

Let the veterinarian make the decision regarding whether it is a good idea to force liquid into the lizard's mouth. As with force feeding, forcing a lizard to take water can be traumatic and painful. The stress contributes to the skink's malaise, and it can weaken the skink's immune system. Forcing anything into a skink should always be considered as a last resort.

### 8) Diarrhea

For the most part, your skink's stool should be solid. However, every now and then, most skinks suffer from a little bit of diarrhea, where their stool is far more runny and watery. Much like with humans, most of the time this is not a serious condition. A single runny stool is nothing to worry about, but if it continues to go on, it is something that needs attention.

It is worth your while to examine any stool that looks unusual. For example, if you see any small specks that look like eggs, or anything moving in the stool, your skink has parasites. If they are at the stage where they are breeding inside your skink's body, it is time to talk to a veterinarian and to sterilize everything in the cage.

Firstly, take a look at what you are feeding your skink. Diarrhea can come from a diet that is too high in wet, sweet fruits. Skip the mango and the oranges for a while, and instead concentrate on feeding your skink food that is comparatively bland and solid. Stick with things like squash, and skip the mice for now. Shredded white chicken breast can help your skink's gastrointestinal tract get back into order.

If you notice that your skink has been having diarrhea more than three times in a row, it is time to seek out the advice of a skilled veterinarian.

## 9) Constipation

Skinks are just like humans in that sometimes, they have to deal with gastrointestinal upset. Skinks typically defecate once after eating, usually within 24 hours. If you notice that your skink has not defecated in a few days, you need to start paying close attention. For the most part, constipation in skinks is no more serious than it is in humans, but every now and then, something more serious is going on.

Start by checking on the conditions of the skink's enclosure. You may find that the humidity has become too low, or you may find that the bulb in the heat lamp is flickering, dropping the temperature. Skinks need a certain temperature in order to digest their food, and constipation can result if the cage is kept too cold.

First, start by touching your skink's stomach. If you notice something hard in the skink's belly, you need to take it to the veterinarian right away. An impaction occurs when there is something that the skink can neither digest nor pass in its belly, and it can be an issue that is fatal very quickly.

If you cannot feel any sort of hardness in the skink's belly, fill a tub with a few inches of warm water and simply bathe it for thirty minutes. As you do so, stroke your fingers down the skink's belly, moving from throat to the anal vent with a firm touch. This helps soothe the skink, and it also might loosen the stool that is inside the animal's body.

After the bath, if the skink has not defecated within 24 hours, contact a veterinarian for your next course of action.

## 10) Dragging Rear Limbs

It is always a little distressing to see your pet lose some of its functionality, and one common problem seen by new reptile keepers is a skink that starts to drag its rear legs behind it. Perhaps you are simply noticing that your pets rear limbs are not moving as quickly as the front limbs, or perhaps your lizard leaves drag marks from its feet and its tail behind it. In either case, it is a situation that warrants some attention.

In some cases, dragging hind limbs can be a result of paralysis due to a back or a spinal injury. If there is an obvious wound or you find that the issue started to occur after a fall or some other kind of mischance, take your skink to the veterinarian. There may be a treatment to restore functionality, and the veterinarian can advise on further action.

Dragging rear limbs might point to metabolic bone disease. While dragging rear limbs might be the first issue that you notice, constipation might also be an issue, as are seizures. Depending on the state of the lizard, you may find that it is also extremely moody. A lizard that was once happy to be held may end up being much more snappy, and one that was relatively bold might spend all of its time in its hide. Metabolic bone disease is a fairly varied condition, but in this case, the answer is as simple as putting your lizard in the sunlight for a few hours. There are many people that feel that skinks require a daily dose of daylight, and though some skinks seem to get along fine without it, it cannot be denied that many cases of metabolic bone disease are straightened out simply by taking the lizard outside.

When you go to take your lizard outside, you will find that it is important to keep track of it. Do not simply release it into your backyard and let it roam. Even large lizards like blue-tongued skinks can get lost in medium length glass, and given that they can escape from poorly latched cages, they can absolutely get out of the average property surrounded by a chain link or wooden fence. Some people choose to allow their skinks to roam while they watch them carefully, while other people prefer to carry their skinks and keep them on their laps when they venture outside.

## 11) Calcium Deficiency

Just like humans, skinks have nutritional requirements that cannot be met by eating one thing. A calcium deficiency is a serious problem that can affect your skink if you do not feed it properly, and it is one of the most common issues seen in skinks that have been rescued or abandoned. In the wild, skinks eat a wide variety of food that prevents this condition, but when a skink is kept as a pet, it is up to the owner to make sure that the skink's dietary needs are being met.

There are several signs that your skink might be suffering from a calcium deficiency. A calcium deficiency can make a skink slow and lethargic, and on top of that, it can also make the skink more prone to injury. Skinks with severe calcium deficiency often break their toes or their legs easily, and before that, they may move around very slowly, as if they are nervous about hurting themselves. You may feel the skink twitch or shiver when it is being held, or you may feel bumpy protrusions along the spine. Many skinks with a lack of calcium in their diets also have jaws that feel loose or soft to the touch.

When you realize that your skink has a calcium deficiency, the best thing to do is to double check that you are giving it the right amount of calcium in its diet. Captive bred mealworms and crickets do not have the nutrients that they need, and the solution is to either gut load these creatures or to dust them with a calcium or multivitamin supplement, as is covered in the Basic Care section.

Another factor in a skink's calcium intake is the type of light that it is getting. In the Basic Care section, florescent light was recommended, and one reason that this was so important was due to the fact that without this kind of light, skinks, particularly diurnal skinks, are unable to metabolize the calcium in their bodies. Check the light that you are using for your skink, and make sure that it is strong enough to keep your animal well fed!

In extreme conditions, your skink might require calcium salts or some other form of calcium that is easy to ingest and which can get into the skink's system fast. This is where a veterinarian can step in and help your animal get the proper dosage that it requires.

## 12) Nail Clipping

Nail clipping is a practice that is somewhat controversial in reptile keeping circles. Some say that it is a basic part of skink care, while other people say that it is not natural and that it should never be done at all. Each reptile owner must make this decision for himself or herself.

In the wild, skinks wear down their nails naturally. They walk on the ground, they climb and they scuttle away from predators. Even the largest and most luxurious enclosure is not like roaming around in the wild, and skinks in captivity simply do not have the same kind of activity level as skinks in the forests or the deserts.

As a result of this factor, captive skinks never have the opportunity to wear down their claws. While small skinks can just barely scratch your skink, blue-tongued skinks are among the largest skinks routinely kept as pets, and these skinks can leave you quite scratched up if their nails are long and sharp.

Some people get by quite well by simply putting more rough matter in their skinks' enclosures. Instead of choosing wood and decorative rocks that are very smooth, they instead use wood with bark attached and rougher rocks. This is a good way to get your skinks' nails to wear down to a natural level.

If you want to try to cut your skink's nails yourself, you will need a towel, a set of clippers, a dish of cornstarch and ideally a friend. The clippers that are used to clip a lizard's nails are the same ones that are used to take care of dogs' and cats' nails. They are designed to account for the sharp curve in the nails of animals, a curve that is lacking in human nails. However, if your lizard is small enough, you can get by with human nail clippers. Ideally, you will reserve a set of nail clippers for your lizard due to issues of salmonella and contamination.

Start by rolling your skink up in a towel so that all limbs are restrained except for the one that you are going to clip. Have your friend hold your skink steady as you clip away only the very tip of the skink's nail.

Like all lizards, the skink's nail has a blood vessel in it. If you clip this blood vessel, the skink will bleed. This is very easy to do if you have never clipped your skink's nails before, so be very, very careful.

If you nick the blood vessel, immediately dip the skink's bleeding nail into the dish of cornstarch. This prevents the wound from bleeding further. Alternately, you can swipe a Q-tip through the cornstarch and dab it against the skink's wound.

Some people choose to clip all four of their lizard's feet at once, while others prefer to give their lizards a little more time. If your lizard is particularly nervous or fretful, it might be worth your time to simply clip one foot every day.

Instead of clipping their pet's nails, some skink owners decide that they would rather file them. Filing is more tolerable for some lizards than clipping is. You can use a regular nail file to do so, and this is something that does not run the same risk as nicking the blood vessel in the claw with a pair of clippers.

Use your best judgment when it comes to caring for your lizard's claws. If the claws are not a problem for you, just leave them alone!

# Chapter 10) Parasites

Parasites are small insects and invertebrates that either live in, on or around your skink. While most of the parasites that skinks deal with cannot be passed to humans and other pets, it is still important to take care of this frustrating issue as soon as you see it. Spending time with your skink on a daily basis and checking its condition regularly is one of the best things that you can do to stay on top of this fairly common problem.

## 1) Internal Parasites

Internal parasites are typically worms that end inside the digestive tract of your blue skink lizard. These worms can strike blue-tailed skinks or any other type of skink at all, and when you are keeping blue-tongued lizards as pets, you need to know how diagnose them and what must be done to treat them.

The symptoms of internal parasites can be subtle at first. The first sign that your skink has internal parasites is typically weight loss and a poor appetite. A skink that was formerly a good feeder may simply turn around and refuse food out of nowhere. Its skin may look slightly saggy, and it may start regurgitating the food that it does eat. Check the skink's stool to see if there has been any change in color or odor, especially if the stool is watery instead of solid.

If your blue-tongued skink is dealing with internal parasites, the first thing that you should do is to make sure that you have isolated it. Internal parasites are very contagious, and if you are housing your skinks together, you need to keep the infection from passing to your other animals. If you are keeping your blue skinks individually, you can simply clean the cage very thoroughly. Get rid of all of the old bedding, clean the cage with very hot water and sterilize the food bowls and water bowls. Check the cage for waste a few times a day, and if you see any, remove it at once.

If you think that your skink has internal parasites, typically what is required is a dose of dewormer. This type of medication is fed to your skink anywhere from once to three times a day depending on what course of treatment your vet requires.

While there are commercial dewormers for reptiles in the pet stores, you will find that they are typically fairly vague about what kind of dosage you should give your skink or even what kind of skink the dewormer is meant to treat. Instead, it is important to go to the veterinarian's office to get the right medication, the right dosage and the right method of treatment for your animal.

In most cases, you will receive the medication in a liquid form, and then it can be forced into your skink through an eyedropper.

One thing that many reptile keepers do when they first bring home a new specimen is to have its stool checked for worms. It is often a good idea to do this early on to make sure that the skink that you have purchased is healthy and that it will not pass on any diseases to the rest of your reptiles.

Remember that a veterinarian is the only professional who can check your lizard for worms. This is not something that you can do on your own. You should also not preemptively treat your pets for things that you are not certain that they have. Trying to dose your pet with a medical treatment that it does not need can be harmful or even fatal.

## 2) External Parasites

External parasites are typically insects that can arrive in a previously clean enclosure through the addition of a new animal or an infected bundle of bedding. Some common external parasites that often affect skinks include ticks and mites, and though they are fairly straightforward when it comes to treatment, you will discover that it is something that requires a great deal of meticulous care.

When you discover that there are external parasites on your skink, start by disinfecting the cage. Place your skink in a clean, temporary holding container, and get rid of all of the bedding. Given the fact that your skink may have been infected by the bedding, it is often a good idea to simply get rid of that entire bag of bedding and buy new ones. Then remove all of the bowls and hides and wash them with hot water if possible.

If you keep wooden toys or hides, it is usually a good idea to simply throw them away, as it is far harder to sterilize untreated wood. If you really want to keep the wooden items, you can place them in a plastic resealable bag, and then place the bag in the freezer for two weeks. Finally, scrub out the tank with very hot water before you replace the bedding, the bowls and the hides.

When you are dealing with ticks, you will find that they are round, brown specks that are most commonly hiding in the folds of your skink's skin. They can be seen fairly easily, and it is easy to treat them as well. Sit with your blue-tongued lizard pet in your lap and start looking for the ticks. They may look like a flat and shiny scale when they have just latched on, but when they have fed off of your Australian blue-tongued skink, they will be nearly spherical.

Use a Q-tip dunked in methylated spirits on the tick, and then use a pair of tweezers to grasp the tick as close to its head as you can. Then pull the tick away from the body of the skink. Even if the head of the tick is still attached, it will be removed at the animal's next shed.

Mites, on the other hand, are a little harder to notice. They are smaller, and it might take you some time before you notice them crawling on your lizard's skin. When you go looking for blue-tongued lizard information, you will often find reptile strips that are designed to kill the mites.

Essentially, these strips are placed in an enclosed plastic container with just a few air holes in it, and then the skink is placed in the container with the strip for a certain period of time. The size of the strip and the amount of time that the skink needs to stay in the container will vary depending on the size of the animal. The strips are readily available from most pet stores, and they are fairly inexpensive.

## 3) Preventing Parasites

Parasites are frustrating problems that can happen to even the most fastidious of reptile keepers. When you learn that you have parasites, you need to take the time to treat the issue, but of course it is far better if you never have to take them on at all.

Perhaps the most common way that parasites can come into your reptile's enclosure is through the bedding. Both aspen and recycled wood pulp bedding can carry parasites, and in many cases, they may only carry the eggs of the pests in question.

To make sure that the bedding is safe, there are a few things that you can do. First, you can simply comb through the bedding with your hands and your fingers. This will help you stir up any mites or ticks that might be hiding in the bedding. Second, and perhaps more effectively, simply throw the entire bag into the freezer and leave it there for a few days before you use it. This will typically kill any small animals or eggs that are clinging to your reptile's bedding.

Another common way for parasites to get into your home is through new animals. It's always fun bringing home a new pet, but make sure that it spends the first month to six weeks in quarantine. That means that it should not interact with the other animals, and in many cases, it means that you should leave it in a tank that is in another room.

Some people have a quarantine tank set up at all times, as it allows them to isolate animals that they feel might be sick. When you are setting up a quarantine tank, line the bottom of the enclosure with paper towels to make sure that you can inspect the stool for any signs of problems.

Lizards do not really get lonely, so do not think that you are depriving it of company. A quarantine period gives you a bit of time to get to know the new lizard, and if it has any diseases, parasites or illnesses, you will know right away. Let the breeder know right away if anything develops with your new lizard.

Another way to cut down on the possibility of having parasites in or on your lizard is to simply avoid purchasing wild-caught animals. Wild-caught animals are typically not treated in any way before they are sold, and it is fairly common for them to be carrying at least internal parasites.

Ask the vendor where their animals came from, and when they were bred. This is a good way to get to know more about your animals and to prevent parasites from affecting your reptile husbandry.

# Resources

Where can you go to find information on skinks and supplies for these great lizards? Check out some of these great resources for any reptile owner.

http://lllreptile.com/
This is an excellent US source for reptile supplies, and it has been operating for some time.

http://www.anapsid.org/
Anaspid.org is one of the oldest sites on the web for reptile information. The information is clear and professionally presented, making it the perfect place to go to look for answers about your reptile problems.

http://www.anapsid.org/societies/
This is Anaspid.org's list of reptile-loving organizations sorted by area. Sometimes, it just helps to talk to someone in person.

http://www.anapsid.org/vets/#vetlist
This is Anaspid.org's list of recognized veterinarians who deal with reptiles. Their list is sorted by country and has entries for both the US and the UK.

http://www.reptilechannel.com/
This is a US-centric reptile resource site with places to find breeders, updates on legal issues concerning reptiles, and an active community.

http://www.exotic-pets.co.uk/
Open since 2005, this family run shop has an excellent reputation as a good place to purchase exotic reptiles of all types.

http://www.888pets.co.uk/
This reptile resource site centered in the UK has good reviews and a wide variety of goods available.

http://www.kingsnake.com
One of the oldest reptile sites on the Internet. Come to talk about your favorite skinks, to find out about new trends in reptile keeping and check out pictures of everyone else's pets.

http://www.kjreptilesupplies.co.uk/
KJ Reptiles is an excellent choice when you are looking to purchase high quality supplies for your skink in the UK.

# Index

CPSIA information can be obtained
at www.ICGtesting.com
Printed in the USA
BVHW091535251118
533944BV00002B/394/P